LADY SAPIENS

Breaking Stereotypes about Prehistoric Women

Thomas Cirotteau
Jennifer Kerner
Éric Pincas

Translated by
Philippa Hurd

With illustrations by
Pascaline Gaussein

HERO, AN IMPRINT OF LEGEND TIMES GROUP LTD
51 Gower Street
London WC1E 6HJ
United Kingdom
www.hero-press.com

Lady Sapiens first published in French by Les Arènes in 2021
This translation first published by Hero in 2022

© Les Arènes, Paris, 2021
This edition is published by arrangement with Les Arènes in conjunction
with its duly appointed agent Books And More #BAM, Paris, France

Translation © Philippa Hurd, 2022

The right of the authors and translator to be identified as the authors and
translator of this work has been asserted in accordance with the Copyright,
Designs and Patents Act 1988. British Library Cataloguing in Publication
Data available.

ISBN: 978-1-91505-478-4

CONTENTS

Lady Sapiens

Key Dates and Evidence Relevant to the Project

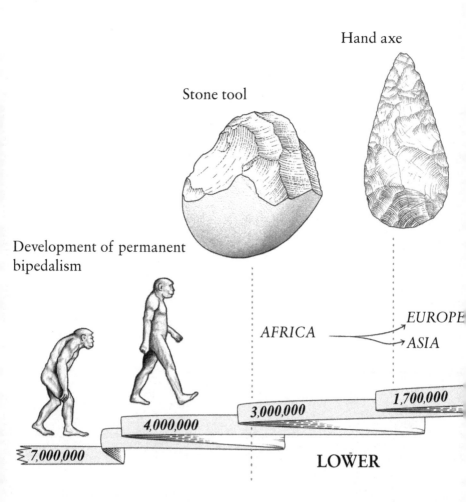

Hand axe

Stone tool

Development of permanent bipedalism

EUROPE

AFRICA

ASIA

7,000,000

4,000,000

3,000,000

1,700,000

LOWER

Burial site
Shanidar Cave,
Israel

Burial culture
Sima de los Huesos
excavation site, Spain

Graphic art
Blombos Cave, South Africa

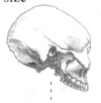

Maximum brain
size

Discovery of fire

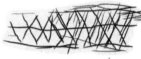

300,000   100,000 BP

1,000,000

P. GAUSSEIN

MIDDLE PALEOLITHIC

PALEOLITHIC

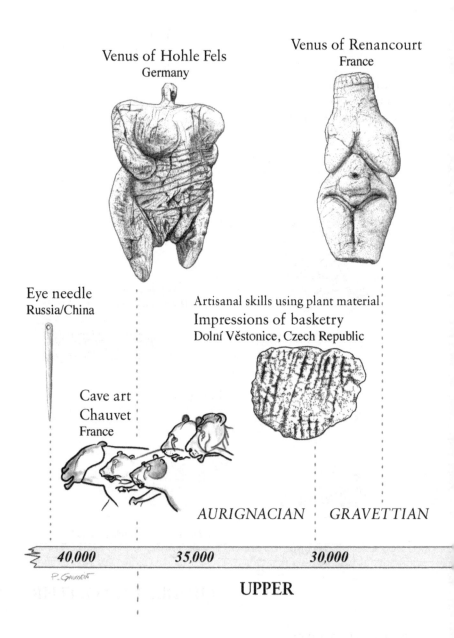

Venus of Hohle Fels
Germany

Venus of Renancourt
France

Eye needle
Russia/China

Artisanal skills using plant material
Impressions of basketry
Dolní Věstonice, Czech Republic

Cave art
Chauvet
France

AURIGNACIAN

GRAVETTIAN

40,000

35,000

30,000

P. GAUSSEIN

UPPER

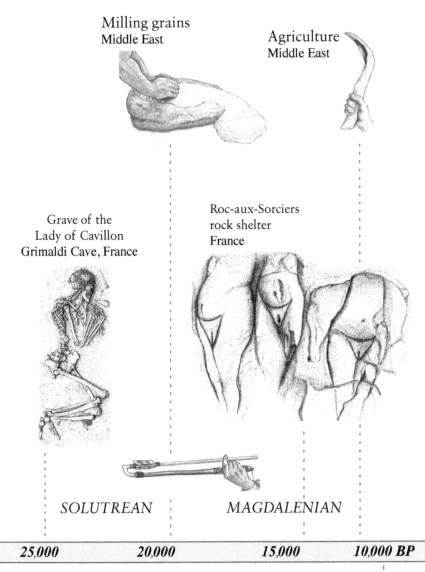

Milling grains
Middle East

Agriculture
Middle East

Grave of the
Lady of Cavillon
Grimaldi Cave, France

Roc-aux-Sorciers
rock shelter
France

SOLUTREAN

MAGDALENIAN

| 25,000 | 20,000 | 15,000 | 10,000 BP |

PALEOLITHIC (Western Europe)

Preface

For a long time, prehistory was written from the male point of view, and when women were mentioned, they were portrayed as helpless, frightened creatures, protected by overly powerful male hunters. Since women have begun to enter the ranks of prehistorians, a different picture has gradually emerged. But between the traditional image of a woman crushed beneath the male yoke and the equally exaggerated vision of a huntress as man's equal, we were missing a more nuanced, rigorous portrait that drew on archaeological sources while taking into account ethnographic approaches. It was with this in mind that I tried to draw up a list of all the archaeological evidence, whether direct or indirect, that tells us about the position of women in prehistoric hunter-gatherer societies. These sources can be the human bones themselves, as well as the objects that were buried in tombs alongside the dead, the prints accidentally left in the clay of the caves, the hands pressed into the walls, leaving the mark of a presence, material remains of skilled work, etc. This overview appeared in a collective work published by Oxford University Press in 2019.*

---

* Sophie A. de Beaune, 'A Critical Analysis of the Evidence for Sexual Division of Tasks in the European Upper Paleolithic' in K.A. Overmann and F.L. Coolidge (eds.), *Squeezing Minds from Stones: Cognitive Archaeology and the Evolution of the Human Mind* (Oxford/New York: Oxford University Press, 2019), pp. 376–405.

I first met Éric Pincas and Thomas Cirotteau in 2018. They had already begun thinking about creating a documentary* on the position of women in prehistory, and I sent them my article, which had then just gone to press. They generously asked me to join them in their work and be their scientific advisor on the documentary, then on the creation of the virtual reality experience that supplements the film, as well as on this book. I accepted this collaboration enthusiastically. This is how my study, which had been published in English and which remained little known in France, became the starting point for the investigation that led to the making of the film with its wonderful title, *Lady Sapiens*. The aim of the documentary and of this book is to make the results of this overview on the position and role of women in prehistory available to as many people as possible.

I insisted that nothing should be imagined or left to chance and that all the assumptions made in the film should be supported by the relevant evidence. It was on this basis that the project gradually took shape. Of course, Éric and Thomas did most of the work, but we consulted together at length to come up with a list of the best specialists in the field who could contribute. This is how they conducted their investigation, which turns out to be the very first on the subject. Prehistorians as well as paleogeneticists, paleoanthropologists, art historians, ethnologists and other specialists have been called upon to contribute. The documentary is structured like a puzzle

---

* *Lady Sapiens*, a documentary by Éric Pincas, Thomas Cirotteau and Jacques Malaterre, directed by Thomas Cirotteau, produced by Little Big Story and Ideacom International, 2021.

or a treasure hunt that can be enjoyed like a real police investigation. Every piece of evidence is pursued, from the excavation site to test-tube laboratory experiments, and the questions are not answered in haste – they are assessed, and any diverging points of view are addressed. The result is a nuanced account, and any argument that's even slightly partisan has been omitted in order to achieve the highest possible degree of objectivity.

This book continues the adventure described in the documentary and takes up the arguments it developed. While remaining highly rigorous, it has been written using clear language in order to be accessible to a large audience of non-specialists. Jennifer Kerner has told the story of the investigation conducted by Éric and Thomas in a way that is both lively and vivid. Both Éric and Thomas read each draft of Jennifer's work, and I personally made sure that every claim was substantiated. Thanks to this highly original collective adventure, the reader should have a more accurate idea of what we can reasonably say about Lady Sapiens today.

But why have we made such a documentary and such a book now? Advances in prehistoric research, which rely on increasingly acute and sophisticated laboratory analyses, are providing answers to mysteries that were impossible to solve a few decades ago. DNA (deoxyribonucleic acid) analysis can, for example, determine the sex of a skeleton in the absence of osteological evidence. And it is now possible to uncover pathologies resulting from work-related stress, an impossible task just a decade ago. In addition, today there are more women scientists, who have naturally broadened their research to include subjects that had been totally ignored, if not looked down upon, by their male colleagues. Activities traditionally considered male, such as hunting and stone-working, took pride of place, in part, truth be told, because they are the tasks that leave behind the most archaeological evidence. Supposedly female activities – preparing animal hides or food, caring for young children – were seen as minor, almost incidental, domestic chores, and attracted little research, no doubt because the first prehistorians were men of the nineteenth century, when women were regarded as subservient, their activities restricted to the domestic field and considered to be of hardly any social value.

Éric and Thomas's project took them to excavation sites and laboratories in France, Germany, Central Europe, the Middle East and the United States. It is not my intention to disclose here the details of this meticulous investigation and the results it produced. In the following pages readers will discover the portrait they were able to create of this woman who lived during the period called the Upper Paleolithic (between 40,000 and 10,000 years ago). They will learn what we can now say about her real role and involvement in daily chores, in the quest for food resources, and about her talents in the field of art and crafts. And finally, they will find answers to questions about her ability to balance her role as a mother with being a full member of the community.

Once the pieces of the puzzle have been assembled, the reader will perhaps be astonished to find that men's and women's roles were not so clear-cut, and that it was cooperation between all members of the group, regardless of their gender or age, which ensured their survival. It is because of them, and especially Lady Sapiens, that we too have survived and are who we are today.

Sophie A. de Beaune
Professor at the Université Jean-Moulin-Lyon III and Researcher at the Archéologies et Sciences de l'Antiquité laboratory, Environmental Archaeology team, scientific advisor for *Lady Sapiens*

Chapter I

THE RETURN OF LADY SAPIENS

On 11 July 2019 at 4:30 p.m., a prehistoric figurine emerged from the sands of Picardy – it was female, six centimetres tall, and it was the first such discovery in France for over sixty years. The Venus of Renancourt – as she was baptized – had come to light, evoking a distant echo of every woman in prehistory. Among the scientific community, emotions ran high, and even the general public appreciated the magnitude of the find. Catherine Schwab, Conservator of Cultural Heritage at the Musée d'Archéologie Nationale in Saint-Germain-en-Laye, finds the magnetic attraction that the object exerts astonishing: 'These images speak to us, move us, challenge us. It is fascinating to see that these objects haven't lost their power over so many millennia.'

This discovery is intriguing. Who were prehistoric women? Did they really look like this figurine? What were their role, their activities and their status within tribes? Did they exist simply to reproduce, or were they great mythical fertility figures? Were they subordinate members of the group or actual providers of food, essential to the survival of their tribe? Could they have been leaders, priestesses or goddesses? These are the many questions that encourage us to unravel the mysteries of prehistoric femininity. The exceptional discovery of the Venus of Renancourt is the start of our journey to discover Lady Sapiens and all her flesh-and-blood sisters who have disappeared from our memory.

Renancourt: A Paleolithic Pompeii

The investigation starts in the city of Amiens, an historic treasure nestled in the valley of the River Somme, a place of contrasts between the Middle Ages and the modern world. It was here in the nineteenth century that Jacques Boucher de Perthes laid the foundations for the first research into prehistory. Work has continued uninterrupted ever since, and archaeologists still plough the furrows of the Renancourt district of Amiens and continue to make many discoveries. Indeed, the Venus of Renancourt takes us back around 27,000 years, its dating made possible by the investigations carried out by scientists at the French National Institute for Preventive Archaeological Research (INRAP).

In 2014, there was an urgent need to begin excavations at the Renancourt site, as urban renewal work risked destroying it for ever – which explains the involvement of the INRAP archaeologists, who intervened even before construction work began. It was during one such survey that Clément Paris, a young archaeologist, made the most extraordinary discovery of his career.

Like a miniature Paleolithic Pompeii, the encampment on the Renancourt site offers the perfect location for studying the lives of our ancestors, as the objects found here have hardly been disturbed since they were abandoned. As scientists unearthed the remains, this miraculously untouched site revealed its day-to-day activities. Clément Paris could scarcely conceal his enthusiasm when he noticed that the conditions were perfect for making exceptional discoveries:

*Gradually, we uncovered the remains that had been aban-
doned by prehistoric people when they left. The surface
occupation site had been quickly covered by a layer of
silt blown in by the wind, which meant that the site was
perfectly fossilized.*

And so with each stroke of the archaeologist's brush, the
ice-age landscape was revealed. The Renancourt site had
been occupied by prehistoric hunter-foragers:* these nomads
moved with the seasons, following large herds of horses,
deer or reindeer. They hunted, fished, foraged for shellfish
and gathered plants for food and to use as medicine. The
Renancourt humans lived in a period we call the Gravettian,
which is dated between 28,000 and 22,000 years ago in Europe,
between the Atlantic seaboard and Western Russia.

In Renancourt, one of these human groups founded a settlement on a hillside in a dry valley, facing a beige chalk cliff.
A highly strategic position, this valley creates bottlenecks in
certain places, which enabled hunters to trap their prey. Hunting
was carried out using long wooden shafts armed at their ends
with a powerful point made of stone or bone to create a spear.
They were thrown directly by hand or using an elongated
rod with a hook at the end, which extended the hunter's arm
and which, by means of a flexible wrist movement, increased
the speed and penetration of the throw. These devices, called
spear throwers, were decorated with delicate, figurative motifs.
Humans thus associated the art of hunting with art itself.

The large quantity of horse bones found at the Renancourt

---

* In this book, we will also talk about 'hunter-foragers'. Unlike the term
'gatherer', which only refers to collecting plants, 'forager' also describes
the collection of shellfish and crustaceans.

site also provide evidence supporting the hypothesis that these were good hunting grounds. To see what the prehistoric horses eaten by humans looked like, we can refer to the images found in the Cave of Niaux in the Ariège *département*. They bear an astonishing resemblance to the magnificent Przewalski's horse, a small animal that can be found today on the Mongolian steppe. They are stockily built, with a large head on a short neck, their coat generally a tan colour, fading to a sandy beige and ending with touches of black on all the extremities (lower legs, tail and muzzle). Of course, horses with other kinds of coats already existed in the Upper Paleolithic, with British geneticists revealing that dappled coats – that is, with darker spots on a grey background – already existed in the case of some types of horse. Moreover, this particular kind of coat was depicted on the walls of the Pech Merle Cave in the Lot *département*, where artists also created hand prints.

The Renancourt encampment was not just perfect for hunting horses, it was also an ideal location for the easy supply of raw materials. Flint and chalk, used in the creation of lots of different tools, are plentiful near the site. Ideal for creating sharp tools, flint was used to cut meat and work on the hides used to make clothes, but it was also employed to fashion objects less essential to survival. Unexpected treasures have been discovered in this time capsule, testifying to a sophisticated culture.

It all started in July 2014, when Clément Paris and his team unearthed the first blocks of chalk. He didn't yet know that he had just excavated some real archaeological gems. The first of these beautiful naked figurines was indeed about to reveal itself...

It was the third day of excavations... The first Venus looked like a shapeless lump of chalk... We decided to extract the block of sediment, and it was during our detailed examination in the laboratory that this figurine appeared before our very eyes... To this day it's the largest figurine that's been found in the settlement – it's twelve centimetres tall. We didn't expect to find this!

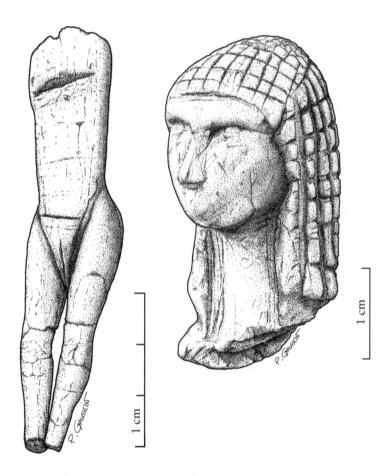

Venus impudica (Laugerie-Basse rock shelter, Dordogne) and Venus of Brassempouy (Grotto of the Pope, Landes), both sculpted from mammoth ivory.

The Venus Factory

A little historical background is useful to get a better understanding of this figurine that Clément Paris describes as a 'Venus'. The term was chosen by the first prehistorians at the end of the nineteenth century to refer to 'antediluvian' representations of scantily clad women. Over one hundred and fifty years of research, nearly a hundred of these figurines have been found, from the shores of the Atlantic to the high mountains of the Urals. Although stylistically very different – whether slender, crude or obese – these women carved in stone, ivory or bone share common characteristics. Their feminine attributes – hips, thighs, chest and pubic triangle – are clearly marked, while their limbs are barely depicted. Often missing a mouth or eyes and tilted slightly forward, the heads are a little out of proportion to the body, if not completely absent. The figurines measure between 1.5 and 22.5 cm in height, averaging around 10 cm. Their use remains a mystery. Some have perforations that suggest they were hung up inside dwellings or perhaps worn as a necklace. Other, more imposing figurines have been interpreted by some as lewd representations or, by contrast, as images of powerful deities. Can the Renancourt site provide clues to a better understanding of the symbolism of these female figurines?

The discovery of the Venus of Renancourt's manufacturing workshop is important, because the number of known workshops of prehistoric artists can be counted on the fingers of one hand, for example the Russian sites of Kostenki and Avdeevo and Dolní Věstonice in the Czech Republic. The Grotto of the Pope at Brassempouy, in the Landes *département*, was also considered to be a workshop because of the large number of figurines found there and the fact that two of them were carved from same block, which seems to prove that they were made locally. However, the excavations carried out in the 1890s were poorly documented, the exact location of the remains was not marked on maps, and any workshop waste was not preserved or even noted by the archaeologists of the time, who were more interested in the beautiful objects they had found. Now, at Renancourt, such small scraps rejected by the artist have been carefully identified and preserved.

Over five years, Clément Paris and his team unearthed about fifteen more or less complete or broken Venuses. All bear the marks of having been worked and fashioned. But the highlight of the discoveries came in July 2019.

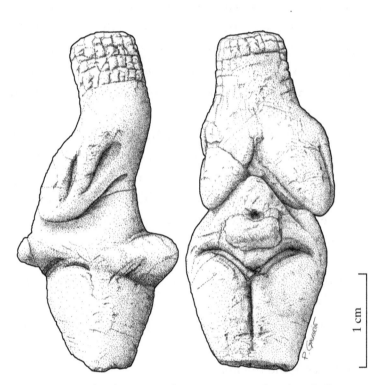

An example of a Venus of Renancourt, sculpted in chalk.

The team discovered the piece that would become the icon of the site: the Venus of Renancourt, a six-centimetre figurine, delicately sculpted in chalk, with anatomical details such as prominent breasts and plump buttocks, completely in accordance with the appearance of figurines from this period dating from 27,000 years ago.

Each Venus of Renancourt has a unique morphology. The most famous of them wears a small checked cap that she seems to have borrowed from Austria's Venus of Willendorf or France's Venus of Brassempouy (see p. 17). The backside of the very first figurine unearthed in Renancourt is so generous that it seems like a pedestal supporting the young woman, whose upper body is frail and elegant. In the case of all the figurines, 'the female attributes had been emphasized by the artist. Magnificent breasts are accentuated, with exaggerated buttocks extending backwards,' says Clément Paris, gesturing voluptuously.

To complete the series, isolated fragments make up a few body parts that have been completely dismembered: a plump belly with the navel clearly visible or a pubic triangle clearly marked between two generous thighs. The lucky man who discovered these priceless remains proudly highlights the magnitude of this find:

These Venus figurines are iconic objects in prehistory, but they had been unknown to the whole of north-western Europe, until we discovered them... And thanks to this exceptional site, we have doubled the number of Gravettian Venuses found in France.

But that's not all. The presence of lots of fragments found in a small space suggests that Renancourt was undoubtedly an artists' workshop – a rare piece of evidence.

The first thing that gave us the idea of a manufacturing workshop was the number of figurines... Fifteen Venus fragments, that's a lot! The second set of clues is the discovery of amorphous chalk fragments that bear the trace of tools. This is waste produced during manufacture, falling from the block as the Venus is created. Finally, we managed to determine that the chalk comes from the cliffs located in the immediate vicinity of the site.

So the Amiens site produced solid evidence to support the workshop hypothesis, namely several half-finished Venus figurines and others abandoned as a result of accidental breakage. Archaeologists also observed tool marks on the surface of the soft chalk: the fact that these waste fragments were saved suggests a piece of unfinished work. Thanks to up-to-date analytical methods, the gestures and tools used by our ancestors to give birth to the Venus of Renancourt will soon come under expert microscopic examination and reveal all their secrets. The photographs, meanwhile, have already told their story. By skilfully applying filters to the digital images, scientists have detected traces of red pigments on one fragment. Clément Paris is thrilled by such a discovery: 'One of the statuettes was painted on the bust using ochre... This specimen has been extremely well preserved, even after 23,000 years in the ground.'

The presence of ochre on prehistoric Venuses has been found on other figurines, such as those discovered at Kostenki in Russia, Willendorf in Austria, Dolní Věstonice in the Czech Republic and Laugerie-Basse in the Dordogne, where the very first figurine, called the *Venus impudica*, was discovered in 1884 (see p. 17). The presence of this mineral dye may have served several functions. The first is obviously to add colour to figurines made of monochrome materials. Ochre was deployed extensively to this end on the walls of prehistoric caves: it is therefore possible that it was also used to create patterns on the sculptures. However, we might consider another function. Ochre is an abrasive material which can therefore smooth the surface of an object. Either way, the presence of this dye proves that we are dealing with works of art that have been given a particular kind of finish.

Other sophisticated examples have been excavated at the site. While the artists of the time were more likely to represent women naked, Clément Paris discovered that the Renancourt artists also knew how to fashion delicate personal ornaments: 'We were incredibly lucky to discover some decorative pieces. Some are made from pieces of fossil, in particular turritella fossils.'

Turritellas are pretty, corkscrew-shaped fossilized sea-shells which were collected painstakingly and possibly sewn onto clothing. Clément Paris does not accept the hypothesis that they were made into necklaces or bracelets, because they do not bear the characteristic signs of wear or friction. He points out that these fossils came from a distant quarry at least 100 kilometres to the south. Taking such an amount of time to find them suggests that personal ornamentation was a serious concern for our ancestors. These delicate decorative pieces attest beyond doubt to the sophistication of these ancient humans' personal ornaments. Their jewellery box also contained other decorative elements: at Renancourt, Clément Paris discovered 'chalk discs painted with ochre and made directly on site in the same way as the figurines'.

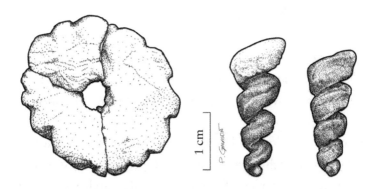

Decorative piece carved from chalk and two turritella
fossils found at the Renancourt site.

With a diameter of three centimetres, these discs have a
hole in the middle and are decorated around the edge with
small notches so that they look like daisies. Some of the
discs were broken during their manufacture, while others
were completed and others were found half-finished. The
remains of these different stages of manufacture show that
the Renancourt artists were very versatile.

Perforated discs are well-known Upper Paleolithic items.
Some of them have been interpreted as optical toys – hung
from a fibre, as the discs are spun round, figures painted or
engraved on them come to life, like the dancing chamois
found at the Laugerie-Basse site. However, it seems that the
Renancourt discs were sewn onto clothing worn by women,
men and children, clothes that were in no way inferior to
ours, as the elegant necklaces, belts and magnificent bracelets
decorating the naked bodies of the Kostenki Venus figurines
prove.

Casting off the Clichés

Prehistory was born as a discipline around 1860, and pre-historians mapped their own models of society and way of life onto those of prehistory. This made women invisible.

In order to understand how the clichés that have influenced our vision of prehistoric society developed, we must start with this fact, as Marylène Patou-Mathis, Research Director at the French National Centre for Scientific Research (CNRS), reminds us. In the late nineteenth century, voluptuous female figurines were objects of fascination for prehistorians and became the focus of their discourse on femininity during these ancient periods. The first archaeologists interpreted them as just figures representing the fertility goddess. Apart from this supposedly divine image, women were quite simply absent from the grand narrative of prehistory or relegated to a subordinate role.

Indeed, during this time, everyone was assigned their particular place. Moreover, the Bible weighed heavily on the image of women and their position in society. Reduced to the role of 'eternal minor' (as defined by the Napoleonic Code of 1804) the 'sinful' woman was supervised from birth to death, passing successively from the care of her father to that of her husband and sons. The scientists who discovered the ancient human world quite naturally placed man at the heart of their working hypotheses. After all, wasn't that how the world had worked since the dawn of time? This is what seems to be suggested by the earliest ancient written sources and the great Greco-Roman myths that had such an influence on Enlightenment society. But this took no account of the evolutionary millennia that preceded the emergence of these civilizations and which perhaps corresponded to mental and societal constructs that were different from our own. For Marylène Patou-Mathis, there is no doubt that 'male domination is a construct – it is not intrinsic to the human species'.

In this way, in the nineteenth century, an image of prehistoric society was established based on the dominant forms of representation of the time, as Sophie A. de Beaune, Professor at the Université Jean-Moulin-Lyon III, emphasizes:

We have to imagine ourselves in the nineteenth century, when women were not highly regarded. They spent their time most often at home, while it was men who had an important economic and social role, and therefore, quite naturally, people imagined that it was the same in the Paleolithic, that man-the-hunter was the one who had finally brought progress to the human species, and that it is thanks to the highly prestigious hunting of large mammals that we have got to where we are today. And at that time women are completely forgotten... We don't talk about women, or else, if we talk about them, we imagine them looking after the home and taking care of children.

Representations in museums and the entertainment industry encouraged contemporary prejudices and helped to publicize these reductive ideas. We might recall, for example, a diorama at Paris's 1889 World's Fair depicting a Cro-Magnon dwelling: thirty-two million visitors marvelled at the famous 'Cro-Magnon man' accompanied by two beautiful women who looked like fashion models and were dressed in simple skirts, their breasts on show to all.

Equally, the Academic painters of the time, who produced works derogatorily referred to as *art pompier* and were the arbiters of taste for official art, seized with relish upon the clichés propounded by scientists. Indeed, from 1880, scenes of prehistoric life became a fashionable artistic genre. Large oil paintings of the period offer a pitiful view of ancient human communities, with ape-like figures decked out in rags, huddling together and fighting for their survival. In such scenes of everyday life, women were represented as particularly timid. Subject to male protection for their livelihood, they were often depicted gazing pleadingly or admiringly at their brave hunter. Often the woman was shown being set upon by a clutch of children who impede her movements and confine her to the domestic sphere. As the journalist and art critic Élisabeth Couturier stresses: 'Paintings such as *Prehistoric Hunt* or *Two Mothers* by Léon Maxime Faivre or *Dangerous Encounter* and *A Rape in the Stone Age* by Paul Jamin were created for bourgeois living rooms. The artists are thus disseminating the values of the bourgeoisie – the housewife and the loving mother. Looking at these paintings, we can learn much more about the relationship between men and women in the nineteenth century than about prehistoric times.'

Michèle Julien, Research Director Emeritus at the CNRS, drives home the point, recalling how unrealistic this vision is, given scientific knowledge on the subject:

The realities of life for prehistoric women are necessarily far removed from the nineteenth-century cliché we were given. Anthropological research has shown that, among all contemporary hunter-gatherers, women perform lots of activities – they are not sitting by the hearth breastfeeding the baby all day, waiting for food to be brought to them.

But the damage had already been done: Academic artists left a lasting impression on the minds of the general public. These images dominated the imaginations of filmmakers, creating screenplays full of stereotypes in twentieth-century films. Buster Keaton's 1923 feature film, *Three Ages*, launched the slew of popular clichés concerning women in prehistory, although Keaton was casting an ironic eye over contemporary male attitudes. Keaton shows us a woman who is fragile, wears too much make-up and dresses in simple animal skins, allowing herself to be dragged by her hair into her cave like cattle or a mere object.

In the 1950s, prehistoric women became peroxide blondes, sensual objects of desire, scantily clad and systematically sexualized. Don Chaffey's 1966 film *One Million Years B.C.* pushes this eroticization to its limit – embodied by sex symbol Raquel Welch. Welch would remain associated with this image in popular culture to this day. Of course, women are now represented as more active and less limited to the maternal role. Nevertheless, they remain secondary characters. The plot is obviously driven by a male hero, and the actresses are chosen according to the contemporary criteria of beauty. Only Alain Chabat's film, *RRRrrr!!!* which was released in the early 2000s, changed the joke by featuring a 'virile' woman, who is far from elegant and mentally weak, as the partner of a skinny man. Intentionally underscoring his almost extreme bias, Chabat places the appreciation of the woman's relative beauty at the heart of the debate. Every time she appears, her husband says, 'Do you know my wife? Isn't she beautiful?' By depicting prehistoric woman as a useless and completely dumb giant, Chabat creates the ultimate caricature.

We might wonder whether popular culture has remained stuck with an image of prehistoric femininity that's now rejected by scientists, especially since gender issues in prehistoric times have only become a topic for debate in the last few decades. In fact, twentieth-century research is still characterized to a large extent by the prejudices of the previous century. The international conference on hunter-gatherers entitled *Man the Hunter*, which was held in 1965 at the University of Chicago, set the tone for the next three decades of research. Its title betraying a very male point of view, this meeting condemned prehistoric women to silence, and hunting was considered a central factor in the discussion of human evolution from the outset. Thus neglected, the subject of women became invisible, even unthinkable. It was only later that the hypothesis of 'women gatherers' was proposed to correct the omission of women and their activities in re-enactments. As Marylène Patou-Mathis says: 'American feminist anthropologists of the 1970s marked a turning point in the history of research concerning prehistoric women.'

Today, many studies are being carried out by prehistorians anxious to restore women to their rightful place in the history of the human species. However, scientists still have some deconstruction work to do in order to overcome the prejudices of academics themselves.

Since the 1970s, male and female scientists have therefore launched a useful debate on the position of women in prehistoric daily life. Far from the idealizing image portraying her as a passive creature, Lady Sapiens can no longer remain hidden behind these distorting fairground mirrors. It is time to paint an objective portrait of Paleolithic woman. No one any more seems to want to take issue with the idea that women have made a significant contribution to the evolution of our species. Moreover, we should remember that the iconic Cro-Magnon, in the valley of the Vézère in the Dordogne – which gave rise to the expression 'Cro-Magnon *man*' to designate our human ancestors – was home to a woman's skeleton. In addition, the archaeological discoveries of recent years lead us back more and more to our own mental constructs. There is thus an urgent need to demand that twenty-first-century research imagine a more realistic Lady Sapiens. To do this, scientists have had to reinvent themselves, exchanging knowledge and engaging in multidisciplinary work in order to understand prehistoric women better. Among these disciplines, ethnoarchaeology occupies a prominent role.

Ethnoarchaeology Comes to the Aid of Prehistorians

In order to offer a new perspective, scientists of the past fifty years have developed new investigative methods to create a better understanding of the past. One of them is called ethnoarchaeology, which makes it possible to put forward interesting hypotheses, as Sophie A. de Beaune explains:

> *Ethnology, that is the study of contemporary populations of hunter-gatherers, can be called upon to form a better understanding of the ways of life of Paleolithic popula-tions. [...] Ethnology extends the range of possibilities,*

as it provides a great variety of solutions that can be customized to each environment. It also enables us to rule out certain far-fetched hypotheses, as they have never been observed in any contemporary or previously existing population.

As we live in an increasingly globalized society where regional characteristics are disappearing, the knowledge we have about the lifestyles of hunter-gatherer populations opens up other perspectives for prehistorians. The incredible diversity of cultures past and present offers new interpretive approaches. Michèle Coquet, Research Director at the CNRS and an anthropologist specializing in the artistic production of West African farmers, emphasizes this cultural richness: 'Seven hundred thousand hunter-gatherers in the Amazon, divided into two hundred different groups, each with their own language and traditions, cosmogony, kinship system... This gives us an idea of the possible diversity among prehistoric populations.'

For many prehistorians, ethnoarchaeology's strength lies in its ability to 'shift our contemporary perspective'. Claudine Karlin, a retired CNRS research engineer, was able to appreciate this in particular during her time spent among nomadic people in Siberia:

When we were thinking about prehistoric butchery practices, we tended to base our ideas on our Western values: it's a mistake. Indeed, a piece of meat with more fat than muscle is not a low-value cut for these populations living in the cold conditions – on the contrary.

Despite its many advantages, making ethnographic comparisons should be done with caution. Michèle Coquet warns against likening contemporary hunter-gatherers to their prehistoric counterparts: 'Contemporary hunter-gatherers rarely live in perfect isolation. They are often in contact with populations who have technologies and means of support that are different from their own. So they're not living "fossils".'

This view is shared by Sophie A. de Beaune: 'It's not about mapping these ethnological data onto archaeological remains, because today's hunter-gatherers are obviously not prehistoric humans.'

Our investigation will therefore not only lead us to explore the past, but also to investigate other directions. From far-flung societies living in harmony with their natural environment to the secrets of our own genes, our journey will take us deep into our common humanity in order to return the women of yesterday and today to a more appropriate position in the history of our species.

Chapter 2

THE REAL FACE OF LADY SAPIENS

Beyond the clichés we have inherited from previous centuries, it is now possible to draw up an accurate composite portrait of Lady Sapiens by first deciphering the archaeological remains, of course – but that's not enough. Fossils were one of the very first materials studied by archaeologists, who were sometimes quick to identify the sex of an individual without any absolute proof. Such was the case of Émile Rivière's 1972 discovery, 'Menton Man', who has since been renamed the 'Lady of Cavillon'. But we'll return to that story later. To find out more about prehistoric women, we must first be able to distinguish their skeletons from those of men. But how do you determine the sex of ancient fossils? Today, other investigative tools are enabling scientists to recreate the real face and body shape of Lady Sapiens in particular. Several solutions exist, and the methodologies are improving more and more as science advances.

Sexing Fossils

Reading the Bones

Bones provide excellent clues. They tell us about populations of the past, revealing the body shape and appearance of our ancestors so that their image becomes more familiar and less distant. Unfortunately, not all bones can determine an individual's sex, and the pioneers of prehistoric archaeology could not make truly reliable diagnoses based on these clues alone.

After decades during which the skull was the main focus of research into the soul and intelligence, the early nineteenth-century archaeologists quite naturally homed in on the bones of the skull in their attempt to understand and identify our ancestors, using such bones to defend evolutionary ideas that we find very uncomfortable today. Naturalists of the time thought that they could read the shape of the skull to see whether its owner belonged to a more or less advanced 'race'. The size of the skull, and therefore the brain, was also considered a good indication of intelligence. Brain size thus indicated which fossils were worthy of being treated as our closest relatives. This reductive and 'cephalocentric' vision created a victim – Lady Sapiens. She had a smaller brain than her male counterparts, indicating her low intelligence, which launched a campaign to devalue her. The skull's volume is proportional to the size of the skeleton, and so it makes sense that the cranial capacity of women is, on average, smaller than that of men. Later on, we will see that this in no way makes their intelligence a foregone conclusion.

So skull size has often been used to identify females in the prehistoric societies being studied. Scientists also relied on the strength of certain muscle insertions and the thickness of the bone above the eye sockets. But these criteria are highly unreliable when we don't know the metric norms of the population to which the individual belongs. Cranial dimorphism, that is to say the differences in skull characteristics between the sexes, is very poorly understood in the case of the Upper Paleolithic, especially since this methodology has an unfortunate tendency to artificially remove older women from the analysis. Sébastien Villotte, a CNRS scientist at the PACEA laboratory in Bordeaux,* explains:

> *It has been shown that the regions of the skull that exhibit sexual dimorphism are affected by age; these studies suggest that women's skulls become more and more 'masculine' as they get older. However, little is known about the mechanisms and extent of this phenomenon.*

So we should reject older studies that claim to be able to identify the sex of an individual from the size of their chin.

The Pelvis, a First Key Indicator

At the end of the twentieth century, scientists began analysing the coxal bone – the hip bone. For a long time, this bone offered anthropologists their only opportunity for knowing the sex of a deceased person, because 'certain hip measurements allow us to determine the sex of the individual', as Sébastien Villotte explains.

The hip bone is the preferred means of performing sex identification because it is the only bone in the human body whose morphology is linked to the possibility of bearing children. Indeed, in women the pelvic girdle has to perform lots of tasks, while the male equivalent has to make do with two functions – walking and supporting the inner organs. Scientists can demonstrate this by showing two complete pelvises (see illustration p. 36). While the difference is imperceptible to the uninitiated, to

---

* PACEA stands for De la Préhistoire à l'actuel: culture, environnement et anthropologie [from prehistory to the present: culture, environment and anthropology].

the scientist it's obvious: one pelvis, honed specifically for walking, is tall and narrow; the other, wider bone offers a circular space in the middle to enable the birth of a baby:

The woman's pelvis suffers two contradictory constraints: that of locomotion and that of giving birth to a child with a large head. The proportions of the female pelvis are very 'constrained': so we can identify their sex very precisely... with over 95–98% reliability.

The problem is that the hip bone is one of the most fragile in the human skeleton – this flat bone is particularly thin, which makes it brittle over time. It often crumbles in the archaeologist's hands as the skeleton is being removed from the grave. To solve this problem, Sébastien Villotte recommends 'taking measures during the excavation, because these bones can be better preserved in situ'.

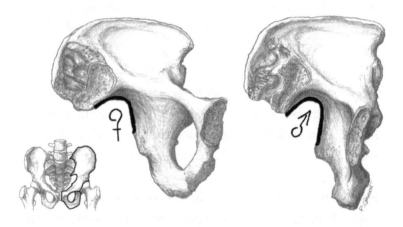

Female hip bone (left) and male hip bone (right).
The angle of the opening reveals the difference.

In order to unify the way measurements are taken and interpreted, a revolutionary methodology was created by anthropobiologists in Bordeaux in the 1990s, namely the DSP method ('diagnose sexuelle probabiliste' or probabilistic sex diagnosis). Using custom-designed software, it guides archaeologists in the field and during laboratory research. Thanks to this valuable tool that Sébastien Villotte uses in his daily work, 'you don't have to have all the measurements to determine the sex. Any combination of four measurements is enough.'

This ingenious technique has just one drawback: it can only analyse adult populations. While in adulthood the hip bone is made up of just one element, it starts out as three bones bound together by cartilage. It is only around the age of fourteen, at puberty, that this cartilage ossifies into one complete bone that archaeologists can measure. And it is from puberty onwards that the female and male pelvises begin to differentiate. In the prehistoric population, the entire 'immature' cohort thus remains of indeterminate sex.

Despite the effectiveness of the DSP method, scientists therefore found they needed to develop another way of iden-tifying the sex of skeletons – it was very frustrating to have to leave out immature individuals. In addition, there were too many burials in which the pelvis had crumbled under the weight of sediment, not to mention the fact that the early archaeologists had excavated several extremely important burials but only kept the skulls. Museum stores are thus full of silent prehistoric skulls whose stories we would love to hear today.

All Ears on the Trail of Our Ancestors' Identity

In the search for other signs of sexual dimorphism, a Franco-African research team focused once again on our ancestors' heads. Using 3D software in his laboratory at Toulouse III-Paul-Sabatier University, Professor José Braga, who is directing this research, has developed a methodology that is about to revolutionize the sexual identification of ancient skeletons:

> We are working with a tool called microtomography, which provides a three-dimensional, cross-sectional image of a scanned archaeological object. By producing this digital reconstruction of part of the skull, we can create a cast using a negative of the organs that were present inside the skull before they decomposed. This is how we've been able to get accurate 3D images of an organ in the inner ear called the cochlea.

The cochlea is indeed bursting with information. This small organ, just over 1 cm long and shaped like a snail, is hidden within the inner ear. As they began working, José Braga and his colleagues observed differences in the twists of the cochlea's spiral canal. In an attempt to find the origin of these different formations, they scanned and modelled ninety-four bones in living patients from France and South Africa, whose age and sex were therefore known. The conclusions emerged quickly: 'The differences are related to gender, not geographic origin.'

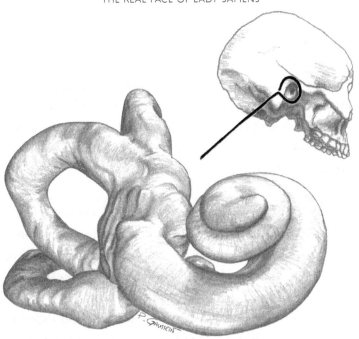

*The cochlea: this internal organ within the ear measures
little more than 1 cm but can, using morphological analysis,
reveal the sex of the individual.*

To the specialist, this is not entirely surprising:

*We were hoping to find morphological variations in the
inner ear, because we already knew that there are differences
in the perception of high frequencies within our species.
When we take physiological measurements on how precisely
we hear these high frequencies, we see that women have
greater sensitivity and greater powers to differentiate these
sounds compared with men.*

The archaeological prospects are huge, since – unlike methodologies that involve the entire skull – scientists do not need to know the morphology of the population in question in order to identify a skeleton's sex. Armed with this good news, the scientists wanted to go further and check that, unlike the pelvic bones, the morphology of this bone did not change as the individual aged:

We studied the cochleas of twenty-two juvenile skeletons in Strasbourg's Anatomy Museum whose sex was known. We then realized that it was possible to identify the sex of immature individuals from the shape of this bone.

Using this new methodology, the scientist can therefore identify the sex of the individual, even when the latter has not reached adulthood. In addition, since the skull is the part of the skeleton with the greatest durability, the chances of finding the cochlea are excellent. The reliability rate is very impressive, with accurate diagnoses on 95% of newborns tested. It's a minor revolution in the world of prehistory, which will eventually enable sex identification in children. 'Unlike DNA analysis, our methodology is not destructive', says José Braga, who is thrilled to have developed a reliable, inexpensive method, which also has the advantage of conserving the specimens for posterity.

In fact, it is essential to avoid taking samples of material from a prehistoric skeleton when the fossils under analysis are old and unique. Nevertheless, the DNA analyses in regular use are the most reliable for studying prehistoric populations and identifying the sex of individuals.

DNA Has Its Own Tale to Tell

DNA analysis can indeed provide accurate identification of the gender of individuals. Professor of paleogenetics, ethnobiologist attached to France's National Museum of Natural History and author of *L'Odyssée des gènes* [*The Gene Odyssey*], Évelyne Heyer is excited by the information these DNA strands can provide:

> *The difference between men and women is easily visible in DNA because they don't have the same chromosomes. Only men have a Y chromosome. In addition, you can determine the sex of a skeleton using just a very small amount of DNA.*

Such genetic material is therefore a valuable commodity, but unfortunately it's fragile and rare. Indeed, 'DNA decomposes a lot in certain contexts – in the tropics, for example – even over short periods of time. And after fifty or a hundred thousand years, it deteriorates a lot, and it's difficult to extract anything from it.' These conservation problems prevent the systematic use of such analyses.

> *Contamination of our ancestors' genetic material through contact with modern archaeologists' DNA is also a major obstacle. There are now techniques to sort ancient DNA from its modern counterpart, such as filtration, which removes all kinds of pollution. But this process of sorting takes time and is expensive. These costs explain why research units have been slow to use DNA analysis in determining sex.*

Improving all the time, these many methodologies have enabled scientists to bring Lady Sapiens and other similar women to the labs' relevant departments for a more extensive examination. Now they aim to cross-reference the data as much as possible to obtain a more precise image of the bodies of these early women. Scientists certainly don't lack persistence in their quest to find out everything about their morphology, their physiognomy, the colour of their skin, their hair and even the colour of their eyes. Today, like no scientists before them, they have succeeded in revealing the true face of these Paleolithic women.

Putting Flesh on the Bones

The Body Never Lies

Nutritional deficiencies, prolonged use of certain muscles, pregnancy: the different aspects of a woman's life are written in her bones. Our bones are continually forming and re-forming to adapt to our movements and needs. To reconstruct the state of health of past populations, archaeologists have been taking the pulse – metaphorically speaking – of these millennia-old patients. Analyses of bones found in archaeological excavations are instructive and indicate first and foremost that in Paleolithic times the entire population was engaged in intense physical activity. Citing one example, Sébastien Villotte offers an initial, important observation:

What we see in the Upper Paleolithic – and generally in all prehistoric populations – is a considerable degree of strength in the upper right and left limbs, in both men and women.

So Lady Sapiens was an all-round athlete. This is not surprising, since she did not have a sedentary lifestyle compared to our own societies. She must have spent time engaging in different kinds of physical activity, providing food for the group in particular. The strength and stamina of these women must have been significant, and their bodies were sculpted accordingly. We must imagine them as muscular women with little excess fat, as their diet of game consisted of lean meat, unlike the fatty meat of the farm animals that would provide food from the Neolithic era onwards.

This provides us with an image that's far removed from the voluptuous Venuses carved in stone or ivory such as the Renancourt figurines. This detail places a question mark over these artworks' ability to shed light on the physique of prehistoric women. Can these figurines really offer a composite portrait? According to the scientists we interviewed, it's a serious mistake to see these figurines as a reflection of women's bodies at that time, and the scientists have been particularly surprised by their very generous figures.

The Enigma of Strong Women

It's impossible that people who led a hunter-gatherer lifestyle would have this type of body shape. I think it could be an expression of certain needs or of the desire to have fat reserves for giving birth and then breastfeeding.

Professor Nicholas Conard of the University of Tübingen sees these curvaceous Venuses as the projection of an ideal rather than as a true portrait. The rolls of fat on their hips, buttocks and stomach are indeed incompatible with their active lifestyle.

It's a point of view shared by Catherine Schwab of France's Musée d'Archéologie Nationale in Saint-Germain-en-Laye, who cites the populations of hunter-gatherers, for whom the artistic evocation of curvaceous women is often linked to a symbolic discourse:

In many civilizations of the past, a highly curvaceous woman was a woman who ate well, which indicated a certain degree of affluence. We can imagine finding this type of criteria in prehistoric populations... The Venuses represent a kind of opulence – even if it's hard to imagine prehistoric women of this size.

This is also the case in today's populations of nomadic herders, such as the Tuaregs of Niger, where female obesity is synonymous with prosperity. But were these plump women as rare as suggested by our image of women as constantly on the move? Let's not forget that our knowledge of the physiology of prehistoric humans is very far from complete. What remains of these bodies of flesh and blood are just a few skeletons that have seldom survived in their entirety. It is therefore possible that the bodies of some of Lady Sapiens's contemporaries had a tendency to store fat.

It has also been suggested that these figurines were representations of women in a particular hormonal state, that they might have been about to give birth or were nursing mothers. Whatever the case, Professor Erik Trinkaus of the University of Wisconsin at Madison notes that 'it is unlikely that the humans of the time never encountered large women, because the distribution of fatty tissue faithfully reflects the anatomical reality of today's overweight women'.

In order to explain why some women developed obesity despite the active life they must have been leading, Trinkaus hypothesizes that this obesity developed during pregnancy. It may also have been a reaction to the physiological stress caused by seasonal migrations. Compensating for this stress, 'extra kilos' might have been gained during certain episodes in their life. It is not impossible that sedentary periods were a time when bodies put on weight to withstand periods of scarcity or strenuous effort. Nevertheless, being obese would have been counterproductive when it was time to move on to the next seasonal encampment. The more obese women would have been slowed down, even handicapped, by their excess weight.

Could it even have been easy for women to put on these excess kilos, given their daily diet? Bones and teeth can help us answer this question: the effects of nutritional deficiency can be detected especially at the extremities of long bones and in tooth enamel. Careful examination of prehistoric skeletons has led to the conclusion that malnutrition was not common in the Paleolithic, but there is no evidence that these women ate more than they needed.

It is therefore very difficult to form an accurate, overall image of the appearance of prehistoric women. We must accept a vision of prehistory as a landscape of biological and social contrasts. What was the norm for a given population could very well be the exception for another group, located a few hundred kilometres away. The composite portrait of Lady Sapiens must thus be recreated each time we focus on a new population from the past. These generously built Venus figurines, however, are far from representing the dominant model.

A Mixed-Race Heritage

The physiognomy of prehistoric populations is the culmination of much interbreeding. Paleoanthropologists (who study the biology of fossil humans) and paleogeneticists (specialists in their DNA) have drawn up a complex family tree. Born in Africa, *Homo sapiens* interbred with several related species.

Évelyne Heyer describes how, at least 50,000 years ago, *Homo sapiens* inherited Neanderthal genes: 'Our species mixed with the Neanderthals in the Middle East when they left Africa... All the humans who migrated to Europe and Eurasia carried in their genome a little bit of Neanderthal – about 2%.'

This 2% is still present in our DNA, providing us with some Neanderthal evolutionary benefits. The immune system of our Neanderthal cousins in particular has contributed to strengthening ours, as well as our resistance to the cold. Lady Sapiens, who lived in the region we now call France 28,000 to 22,000 years ago, was a carrier of this Neanderthal genetic legacy.

It's safe to say that we still haven't identified all the ancestors who have bequeathed us a few of their genes. Research in this area makes it possible to measure the potential of future discoveries. Since the late 2000s, scientists have added a new photo to the family album of the genus *Homo* – the Denisova hominin, discovered in the Altai Mountains of Siberia. Did Lady Sapiens also bear the genetic inheritance of this eastern relative? There is no fossil evidence to say so. Nevertheless, Papuans and Australian Aborigines carry as much as 6% of this genetic material.

Secrets of Skin Colour

The first Homo sapiens *to arrive in Europe 45,000 years ago were dark-skinned, and people in Western Europe retained this dark colour for a long time. It was not until the* Neolithic *period – 6,000* BCE *– that we see a lightening of skin colour among European populations.*

Évelyne Heyer's revelation is surprising, as the reconstructions of prehistoric women we see in museums and popular books rarely have dark skin.

It has recently been discovered that depigmentation has indeed evolved at a slower pace than migration into the territory of Europe. Heyer regards this discovery as unexpected: 'We thought that humans adapted more quickly to a climate with less sunshine than in Africa... Indeed, having a lighter skin colour makes it easier to assimilate Vitamin D in northern latitudes.'

Based on meat, bone marrow, animal fat and fish in particular, the Paleolithic diet naturally contributed to Vitamin D intake and therefore delayed depigmentation. In the Neolithic period, everything speeded up with the appearance of agriculture: as cereals are less rich in Vitamin D, the skin became depigmented to improve its synthesis.

We must therefore imagine Lady Sapiens as a mixed-race beauty who still looked broadly African, with black afro-textured hair and dark skin. But one singular detail emerges around 40,000 BCE that would continue right up to the beginning of the Neolithic period:

10,000 years ago, in Western Europe, all the Europeans we have been able to study have black skin and blue eyes.

Once again, the research results are surprising, and Évelyne Heyer admits that she 'doesn't fully understand the advantage of blue eyes in terms of natural selection'.

The presence of blue eyes is therefore probably the result of sexual selection. Since there is no physiological benefit attached to it, we can assume that blue-eyed partners were considered more attractive, as their lineage became more widespread than the others.

If we close our eyes, we can now visualize the appearance of our prehistoric heroine more intimately and more precisely – tall, muscular, mixed-race with dark skin and blue eyes. But what might have been her position within the tribe? How can we find out what her daily activities were? Scientific advances are coming up with ever more surprising answers that challenge what we thought we knew for certain.

Chapter 3

LIFE, PLEASURE, SEDUCTION

In complete contrast to the bizarre image of wild, shaggy and filthy creatures with a bewildered expression, prehistoric populations have in fact been shown to be extremely sophisticated, both in their art and in their personal adornment. In the Upper Paleolithic, women's bodies – and even men's – were soon enhanced through the creation of particular objects, whether it was elegant clothes, jewellery or body painting. Clothing brought many advantages. In the first place, it offered protection against environmental conditions – especially the cold – but it also provided a means of cultural expression. We should also note that all these creations came about before the invention of eye needles, which would help make clothes fit more snugly and produce ever more delicate forms of decoration. Does this mean that very early on our ancestors preferred aesthetics over function?

As ethnological research shows, personal ornaments are an indicator of an individual's membership of a particular human group. Ornamentation is therefore likely to say a lot about the individual's position within the group: those deemed 'important' by their fellow members often enjoyed lavishly decorated clothing. But that's not all. Ethnologists have even been able to observe forms of amorous display among early populations, expressed through ornamentation:

the exchange of genuinely private messages could indeed take place by gifting particular items of jewellery. Marian Vanhaeren, Research Director at the CNRS, cites the example of 'young Zulu women who make bead breastplates for the men they would like to marry, sending messages through the intermediary of the colours and patterns they use'.

And sometimes it is the men who wear make-up and dance in front of the women to seduce them, as among the Fula people of West Africa. While it may be hard for prehistorians to find the symbols hidden in personal ornaments that are thousands of years old, nonetheless scientists can draw lots of conclusions from studying jewellery. Their initial observation is that prehistoric humans had a definite taste for rare and delicate ornamentation – completely contradicting the notions of the nineteenth-century Academic painters who depicted our ancestors as dishevelled animals, swathed in ragged, uncrafted animal hides.

Magnificent Personal Ornaments

Jewellery seems to have played a significant role in ornamenting prehistoric bodies. The diversity of the ornamentation is enough to make your head spin. Archaeologists have found rows of shells to be worn on various parts of the body, rings, mammoth-ivory bracelets and even possible earrings. At least, this is what is suggested by a split bear tooth that was discovered near the ear of a skeleton excavated at Baousso da Torre II. This site is part of the famous Balzi Rossi cave complex in Italy, which also includes the Barma Grande, Grimaldi and Cavillon Caves. In a burial in the Barma Grande, rows of prehistoric beads were found around the neck of the deceased. Some of our ancestors also liked to wear brace-lets, as found, we assume, in the Grimaldi Cave. Finally, we know of examples of leg bracelets or anklets: the 'Lady of Cavillon', buried 24,000 years ago in the eponymous cave, wears a row of cyclope or sea-snail shells around her calf. The 'Reindeer Woman', engraved on a fragment of antler found at Laugerie-Basse, is also sporting an anklet.

Prehistoric beads are incredibly diverse. Making good use of natural forms, humans collected a variety of shells. In order to add new features to these already unique pieces, the jewellers of ancient times modified the appearance of the shells using different processes which made it possible to change the colour of the ornaments temporarily (by adding pigments) or permanently (by exposing the shells to fire to darken certain areas).

Some of the natural elements used to create personal orna-ments would occasionally run out. The canine teeth of deer, for example, cannot be obtained in great numbers. Indeed, these animals live in woods and forests typical of temperate climates. Now, during the Upper Paleolithic in Europe, low temperatures gave rise to the spread of tundra or almost tree-less steppe. At the same time, deer canines remained highly sought-after. These two upper canine teeth, with their unu-sual, globular, asymmetric shape, were very popular between the Upper Paleolithic and the Neolithic. Their surface was sometimes decorated with geometric engravings – crosses, chevrons or a simple series of evenly spaced stripes. Deer canines were so highly valued that imitations were sometimes made using alternative materials. Similarly, false horse incisors were made out of bone or ivory, creating the first forgeries in history. This detail is important, because it highlights the fact that, already at that time, the scarcity of certain items could encourage craftsmen to make imitations. It is rather startling to think that women living 15,000 years ago may have been obliged to enquire about the authenticity of their bead necklace.

Magnificent pendants were also created, probably intended to be worn alone or as the central element in a composite piece. Craftsmen engraved geometric patterns on stone disks, as at the Mitoc-Malu Galben site in Romania. They also sculpted three-dimensional elements – in an almost Cubist style – as was the case with the famous flat blade-shaped pendant found in the Cave of Brînzeni in Moldova. These jewellers also made figurative pendants. The elegant mammoth ivory carving found in the Vogelherd Cave located in Germany's Swabian Jura and the now iconic Venus of Hohle Fels from Germany bear witness to this.

While women and men of the past used exotic objects that came from a region far away from the place where they lived to make their ornaments – the necklace of the Lady of Saint-Germain-la-Rivière, discovered in the Gironde, is made of Spanish deer canines – they also used items they could access easily. Thus, the inhabitants of prehistoric Italy took advantage of their proximity to the Mediterranean and included sea urchins and fish vertebrae in their personal ornaments.

However, the shapes their creations took were not limited to the use of indigenous resources. Different populations developed regional preferences for certain raw materials that do not necessarily seem linked to their ease of access. So we can see trends varying according to where people lived: wolf and fox canines were popular in Eastern Europe, where elongated shells were also sought after, and deer canines were preferred in South-west France, where globular shells were equally fashionable.

In their search for delicate shapes and textures, our ancestors were also the first feather-workers in the history of fashion, and the feathers likely held a particular significance for both men and women. In the Lady of Cavillon's headdress there's an empty space above the forehead, which archaeologists see as a sign that a perishable material, such as feathers or braided leather, was used. Golden eagle and swan feathers were also used, although it is impossible to know if their feathers were embroidered onto clothes, added to hairstyles or attached to jewellery.

The variety of personal ornaments and the care taken in choosing materials indicate unquestionably that Paleolithic peoples possessed a combination of pragmatism, creativity and an eye for beauty, and that, without a doubt, both men and women wanted to make themselves desirable to others.

Beautifying the Skin

Ornamentation could also be ephemeral when it was applied to the surface of the skin. Francesco d'Errico, CNRS Research Director, has been analysing an iconic prehistoric mineral – ochre. This pigment comes in vibrant shades ranging from deep crimson to sunshine yellow. Its use is deeply rooted in ancient history:

The oldest traces of ochre use in Africa date back 300,000 years. But, in the Upper Paleolithic, this use seems to become more complex. It achieves several kinds of objective… Used on cave walls, ochre is an element in artistic creativity, but it also plays a role in the daily life of individuals.

Traces of ochre can be found everywhere, because it is indeed multifunctional. Ochre is highly sought-after for its abrasive properties, and so it can be used in the preparation of animal hides to tan the leather. Ochre's antiseptic properties protect leather from rotting and facilitate the removal of residual organic matter and small blood vessels. But it's also used in the finishing stages of works of art such as the Venus of Renancourt. Ochre also functions as a prophylactic when applied to human skin, as it protects against the sun and insect bites. As Francesco d'Errico says, for these reasons it's natural for ochre to be used in the daily ablutions of certain populations: 'The Himba women (in present-day Botswana) cover themselves in ochre because the use of water is taboo. Women wash themselves by mixing ochre with fat.'

Ochre could also be employed in limited quantities for very detailed purposes. Francesco d'Errico analysed the microscopic marks on small red ochre sticks found in Porc-Épic Cave in Ethiopia and thinks he has spotted evidence of a very specific use:

We found sticks with several facets produced using different grindstones. Some of them yielded just a few milligrammes of powder. So prehistoric people produced small quantities of ochre, which seems more compatible with symbolic use… such as drawing lines on the face, for example.

It is therefore highly likely that body paintings were made directly on the skin. This use of ochre is not unimportant, since acquiring and preparing it involved a great deal of effort by the entire group. Laure Dayet, a scientist working with the TRACES* laboratory at the University of Toulouse-Jean-Jaurès, has been looking at this special pigment. The minerals are examined under the microscope to understand their properties. To that end, it is now possible to 'determine the atomic composition of different kinds of ochre using electron microscopy'.

Identifying their composition is important, because all geological deposits have their own chemical properties. By cross-checking the analysis of archaeological objects with that of geological samples collected today, scientists can locate the places where prehistoric humans obtained their supplies of raw materials. Moreover, the latter were chosen with great care, continues Laure Dayet:

In the Upper Paleolithic, the selection of rocks to make pigments was very exact. The rocks were chosen for their very fine particle size, making them easier to crush. Prehistoric people also chose almost completely pure iron oxides. They didn't necessarily select raw materials near where they lived, but they could also look for materials more than 50 kilometres from their base camp... That's more than a day's walk away.

In order to stock up on supplies, the groups therefore had to send some of their members out on expeditions. They were also able to establish a long-distance trading network with

---

* TRACES stands for 'Travaux et recherches archéologiques sur les cultures, les espaces et les sociétés' [Archaeological Work and Research into Culture, Space and Society].

other groups to get hold of exotic materials. Whatever the solution, this acquisition was necessarily a costly investment for everyone involved, a process that required organization and know-how.

Decades of trial and error and the transmission of knowledge was necessary in order to master the composition of pigments. Indeed, it was not enough to crush haematite-rich rocks to obtain the material to paint your body or create works of art. Pigment-making is a technical feat that demands knowledge of how to mix several minerals, as Laure Dayet explains:

> *Pigments sometimes contain several different rocks. To colour a surface, you need both colouring power, linked to the pigment, and the covering power of the mineral, as well as a binding substance. If our ancestors wanted to make their mixtures sparkle, they might also have added mica or graphite, etc.*

It is unclear whether women played an important role in this production of pigments. Among the Himba of northern Namibia, it is a woman's job to collect them. But as for prehistoric times, there is no archaeological evidence that enables us to propose an exclusive model suggesting the sex of the individuals responsible for this work.

Francesco d'Errico is convinced of ochre's symbolic diversity, thanks to his years of research into these mysterious powders:

> *Using experiments, we can see that each type of ochre can have a particular function. The ochre for making paint will*

not be the same as that used for tanning hides or the ochre
applied to the body. Different varieties of colour are also
going to have meanings. The body is transformed into a
symbol, just as in the case of personal ornaments.

The use of different types of ochre might relate to a particular status (senior hunter, spiritual leader, herbalist, etc.), a rite of passage (from childhood to adulthood, the union of two people, a funeral rite, etc.) or to seasonal festivals.

Indeed, the skin is a blank canvas that artists across the ages have sought to beautify in many different ways. While the oldest preserved tattoo remains the one found on Ötzi, the famous 5,300-year-old natural mummy found in the Tyrolean ice, Paleolithic women and men already had all the tools and artistic potential to be peerless tattoo artists. Needles made of volcanic rock, like those used in Melanesia over 4,000 years ago, allowed the pigment to penetrate beneath the skin. In the absence of ink – aside from the possible use of squid ink – carbon black was used to create lasting patterns under the skin. Certain geometric marks incised on sculptures have been interpreted as scarifications, and they were already feasible in the Paleolithic, although there are no material traces to prove it in the absence of a mummy older than Ötzi. Such a discovery is far from impossible, as melting glaciers are revealing more and more prehistoric organic remains that have been preserved by the ice.

Adorned with colours, and perhaps also with tattoos and scarifications, the epidermis needed to be looked after. In fact, the skin is the most extensive organ in the human body, a precious and sensitive link between the self and the outside world. An effective barrier against attack by the natural world, it is also a vector of communication between the elements and the individual. The skin is an intermediary we need to synthesize valuable Vitamin D which builds up our skeleton, but it's also the matrix that connects lovers and, later, a mother with her child. It is therefore highly likely that the skin, hair and beards were given special care and attention. Moisturizing balms and other nourishing masks were possibly used, but at present no archaeological trace has been found of this ancient beauty pharmacopoeia, unlike other curative herbal remedies which we will discuss later.

In order to protect their smooth, fragile skin, our ancestors invented something incredible – clothes. The clothes hanging in our wardrobes may seem totally mundane to us, but their arrival in our lives was a real revolution for humanity.

Clothes – and Needles – Start a Revolution

The first garments were being created well before the invention of the eye needle in China and Siberia 40,000 years ago. Indeed, very fine bone awls were all that was needed to sew textiles or tanned hides together edge to edge. As Francesco d'Errico explains, 'The oldest tools for making holes in hides, such as the very thin, heat-hardened awls found at the South African Blombos Cave site, emerged in Africa between 80,000 and 70,000 years ago.'

But what tools have archaeologists got to date when the first clothes appeared? We recall that the genus *Homo* lost their hair a million years ago. Living under the African sun, our ancestor, *Homo erectus*, acquired characteristics such as the ability to walk long distances and endurance. And it was perspiration, a thermoregulatory system activated by the sweat glands, that contributed to the loss of hair all over the body. So for thousands of years our earliest ancestors probably went about naked. The question that taxes scientists is when did the inhabitants of temperate zones start covering their bodies with animal hides or plant material? Unexpectedly, the answer lies in the evolution of a skin parasite that is, to say the least, unpopular, as Francesco d'Errico explains:

The genetics of the louse tell us a lot about the earliest kinds of clothing. Today there exist two types of louse: the head louse and the body louse. A recent study carried out by German scientists showed that this genetic difference emerged 120,000 years ago. From this time onwards [...] a continuity was created between the hair the lice infested and the rest of the body, because people were wearing furs, and so the lice were able to live in the fur as well as on the head.

These two parasites on the human body then each went their evolutionary way, resulting in head lice and pubic lice or crabs.

And so our ancestors began wearing clothes at least 120,000 years ago. However, these early clothes probably didn't fit very well, and it was the invention of the needle that made it possible to create more tailored garments. This stylistic turning point in our ancestors' wardrobe was not a question of mere vanity, but an adaptation to the harsh glacial climate. Indeed, layers of thin clothing are essential for creating good insulation against the cold. The invention of the eye needle was an important step in improving the comfort of prehistoric people's lives. Using meticulous skills, the craftsman first chose the right material – a slender reindeer antler or a long bone – into which he gouged two parallel grooves from which, when they joined at each end, he could extract a thin sliver. The craftsman then just had to scrape and polish the sliver using an abrasive material and perforate it to make a needle with an eye.

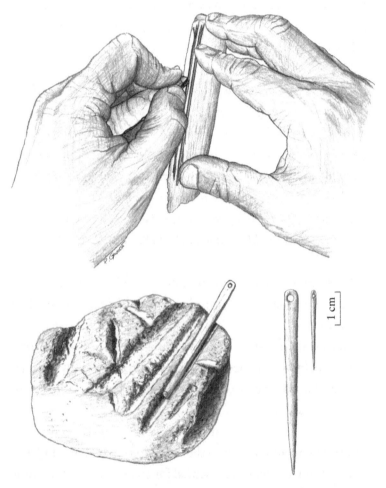

Extracting the matrix of an eye needle from a bone by gouging (top). Polishing using a stone to round off the edges of the shaft. Two examples of finished needles (bottom).

Needles are not just simple tools; sometimes they can be little works of art. As Francesco d'Errico says, 'Some needles are ornate and decorated with ochre. This has nothing to do with function – prehistoric dressmakers were just being creative.'

From the sewing tools to the clothes themselves, prehistoric people combined aesthetics and efficiency even when choosing which materials to use. Animal hides that were de-haired or scraped and then tanned were used to make warmer clothes. Ethnographic studies of the Canadian indigenous peoples who predate the arrival of the settlers show that fur was worn next to the body with the leather on the outside to protect against the elements. The skins were used whole and uncut, so the animals' paws and head must have played an important aesthetic role in the creation of the garment.

Essential for waterproofing the leather and preventing it from going mouldy, tanning could be carried out using various plant, mineral or organic materials, such as deer brains mixed with ochre, manganese or chalk, depending on the desired colour. Varying degrees of suppleness and shades of leather could therefore be obtained depending on the technique – or combination of techniques – and the choice of pelt. The art of making clothes was already very sophisticated.

To meet specific needs, it is quite possible that Paleolithic peoples developed what prehistoric beauty expert Élisabeth Azoulay has called 'aesthetic predation'. Hares, foxes and squirrels were the targets of this kind of hunting. Their fur was used to make clothing more waterproof at the cuffs and in the hood, but it also added aesthetic value to such overcoats.

In some hunter-gatherer tribes in North America, before the arrival of the Europeans, fur indicated a person's status. Hare was worn by children, fox by young women, while old women had a monopoly on lynx.

For more delicate clothing, fabrics made from woven plant matter or animal fleece were used. Obviously, these materials did not survive millennia of being buried in the earth, but surprising evidence has been found at the archaeological site of Dolní Věstonice in the Czech Republic. Fragments of baked clay bear the imprint of woven fabric. According to American archaeologist James Adovasio, an international specialist in perishable artefacts, 'It might be pieces of floor covering or clothing, in some cases it was fishing nets or bags that had been made for hunter-gatherers who lived in Věstonice' (see illustration on page 160). Placed next to the hearth, the clay hardened and fossilized the image of these ephemeral creations.

It is highly likely that the shapes of the clothes were particularly varied: as soon as humans were able to fashion sewing needles, they could create an arsenal of patterns as aesthetic as they were practical.

What might these prehistoric clothes have looked like? It's a safe bet that the bikini proudly worn by Hollywood stars in *One Million Years B.C.* was not yet the height of fashion. Indeed, clothes had to address primarily a practical imperative – protecting the delicate skins of *Homo sapiens* from the effects of freezing winters and scarcely more clement summers. Of course, clothing is not the only possible way of protecting the skin. The Yamanas of Tierra del Fuego in Argentina preferred to cover themselves with seal oil and remained naked, even in sub-zero temperatures. However, it is reasonable to argue that wearing clothes was the most common solution around the world. These prehistoric clothes were severely tested by the temperatures of the time. For example, 12,000 years ago, in the Neuchâtel region, they ranged from 9°C in summer to -25°C in winter. These significant variations must have resulted in seasonal adjustments to Lady Sapiens's wardrobe. According to Francesco d'Errico, to create these collections, prehistoric people needed an efficient sewing kit, including needles adapted to different tasks and different materials:

Beginning 40,000 years ago, needles became more and more varied. At first, there were only large needles, and towards the end of the Upper Paleolithic, we've found needles of very different sizes. This reflects the increasing complexity of activities to do with clothing.

Paleolithic art shows that the items of clothing that made up the outfits of Lady Sapiens and her women friends were varied. Some engraved plaquettes depict human figures wearing a kind of hooded anorak. This type of clothing also features on certain statuettes, including forty Siberian Venus figurines.

In the 1950s, on the shores of Lake Baikal, archaeologists excavated some small mammoth-ivory figurines measuring between 4 and 13 centimetres tall. These Venuses, found at the sites of Buret' (see illustration opposite) and Mal'ta, date from the end of the Paleolithic (21,000–17,000 BCE). At first glance, some of the figures seem naked, but microscopic analyses carried out by Lyudmila Lbova and Pavel Volkov of the Russian Academy of Sciences suggest that the existence of grooves might represent clothes, necklaces and even bags worn on the body. On other figurines, the depiction of the garment is clearly visible, and the deeply cut notches leave no doubt that the artists wanted to represent a thick garment, perhaps made of fur, using different horizontal bands to suggest the many furrows running across their bodies. It is therefore understandable that modern illustrators have drawn reconstructions of women dressed in fur, perhaps succumbing to the very Western fantasy of 'Venus in Furs', as described by Leopold von Sacher-Masoch in 1870. In reality, the patterns on these figurines are more reminiscent of those traditionally used by the Inuit and Native Americans on their parkas. It's also conceivable that they are representations of outer clothing, items worn over a leather and fur outfit as a kind of wind-cheater or raincoat. For this type of clothing, much more delicate materials were used, such as submucosa derived from the internal membranes of animals (like intestines, bladder or oesophagus). These clothes are ergonomic wonders: both light and warm, they also are naturally breathable. Such efficiency can only be achieved with a great deal of effort – the process to manufacture the raw material alone takes three months. Very practical for keeping out the cold and wet, these clothes have a sacred meaning for certain subarctic populations, who believe that such clothing is a concentration of the animal's life force. Shamans wear such clothes in order to communicate with the spirit world.

Venus of Buret', dated to the end of the Paleolithic
(21,000–17,000 BCE), seems to be wearing a hooded anorak.

The various finishes applied to the clothes were as useful as they were aesthetic, for Lady Sapiens must have wanted to please herself as well as others. Buttons, those precious tools for fastening coats and capes effectively, were already familiar inventions. The Italian archaeological sites of Barma Grande and Arene Candide in Liguria have provided some examples. It is also possible that our ancestors used pins: types of large ivory needles that could have been used to fasten clothes have also been found.

The depictions of figures found in the La Marche cave also reveal the existence of elaborate belts. A belt is sometimes even the only item depicted on the body of naked females, as if this piece, worn in private, were the last piece of clothing to be taken off. But it might also have been a very useful accessory for hanging various tools (bag, knife, etc.).

Headdresses were also worn and were represented by cross-hatching found on the heads of many Venus figurines. Some fragments of these caps have even survived. The best example comes from the grave of the Lady of Cavillon, who died 24,000 years ago and was buried in the eponymous cave located under the cliff of Balzi Rossi in Italy.

The skeleton was found wearing a spectacular ornament consisting of two hundred shells and twenty-two ochre-covered deer canines. These elements were probably threaded onto a mesh made of a perishable material, which is now missing (string made of vegetable fibres, animal tendons or leather thongs) but whose presence we can decipher.

What did these different accessories represent in prehistoric societies? Were they indicative of the particular status of those women and men who wore them, or were they fulfilling a sense of aesthetic pleasure, a need for seduction? The latest research provides us with some answers.

The First Status Symbols?

In traditional societies, personal ornaments were an important part of visual language. They enabled the wearers to express many social and economic variables. Solange Rigaud, a scientist at the CNRS, describes the multidimensional nature of personal ornament within human groups:

In the modern societies studied by ethnologists, personal ornaments serve both to encode social information relating to the individual who is wearing the personal ornament and to encode information about the group to which the individual belongs.

Michèle Coquet adds that personal ornaments are also linked to types of body modification, which are very meaningful in a social context:

They pierce their ears and lips: the body is modified to wear personal ornaments. This reveals another function of personal ornaments – that of humanizing. Because humans are seen as 'coming from elsewhere' – they are neither humanized nor socialized from birth – and modifying the body to wear personal ornaments is part of this civilizing process.

Should we imagine that prehistoric people modified their appearance to send messages about themselves and their mental world? For Michèle Coquet, there is no doubt: 'These multiple functions of personal ornament and clothing – utilitarian, concerning identity and one's place in society – exist in all the populations ethnologists have studied.'

In other words, wearing a piece of jewellery will not only indicate which group the individual belongs to, but also what their position is within that same group. This creates different categories of people. Among them, some might be immutable (chief, priest or shaman, for example), others may evolve over the individual's life and through initiation processes. Women of marriageable age, those looking for a partner, mothers, women in couples or menopausal women have a whole arsenal of personal ornaments to display their status and their ambitions. Don't forget that men and children also wore personal ornaments and that beauty was not the preserve of women. Francesco d'Errico is not surprised that 'personal ornamentation is part of the male as well as the female world, as the burials have revealed. Many men buried during the Upper Paleolithic are wearing ornaments.'

The Russian site of Sungir provides a perfect illustration. Some 200 kilometres from present-day Moscow, a lavish funeral ceremony was held 27,000 years ago. Thousands of years later, archaeologists were astonished to discover the grave of a man and a double one, less than 5 metres away, containing two children of indeterminate sex. These high-status individuals had been clothed in elaborate finery for their last journey: fur trousers, chunky boots and various kinds of anoraks, all intricately embroidered with thousands of tiny mammoth ivory beads.

In 2012, when examined under the microscope, the beads revealed crucial information: these sumptuous garments were not just funeral clothes, nor even ceremonial clothing worn only on special occasions, like the wedding dresses that accompany young women into the afterlife but which were worn only once during their lifetime. The beads on these costumes were abraded, revealing that the garments had been used regularly. Prehistorians were amazed that such extravagant clothing might have been part of everyday life. The fact that such clothes were worn daily by some members of the group is an excellent indication of the sophistication of their tastes and way of life. Of course, archaeologists believe that these individuals enjoyed a degree of prestige. It seems hard to imagine the average man and woman displaying so much wealth through their everyday clothing. It is therefore highly likely that this costume was an indicator of hierarchy.

Men were not the only ones to be laid in 'prestigious tombs': archaeologists have also discovered some women buried with their extraordinary jewels. We'll be looking at the burials of these exceptional women in a future chapter.

Be that as it may, all these personal ornaments and clothes are indications of populations whose good taste and sense of beauty were very distinct, and where the desire to seduce must undoubtedly already exist. But is it possible for us today to find out how Paleolithic men and women got together? How can we unravel the secrets of their private lives, the physical bonds that united them to create new life and ensure the longevity of the group? This is a tenuous field of investigation for prehistorians, some of whom are nevertheless beginning to provide accurate answers by using both archaeological evidence and ethnographic observation.

Chapter 4

SENSUALITY AND SEXUALITY

Human sensuality and sexuality are unique. Ethnological and anthropological studies clearly highlight our originality in such matters. But why did the great ape that we are come to differ from our cousins to such an extent? It seems that our uniqueness is to be found first and foremost in our DNA. In the huge phylogenetic tree of primates, our ancestors pursued a singular path, characterised by the separation of our lineage from that of orangutans 20 million years ago, from that of gorillas between nine and ten million years ago, and from that of chimpanzees and bonobos between six and eight million years ago. This path is strewn with major physical and behavioural changes that make us the incredible human machines that we have become. These changes had a significant impact on the way humans imagined and then organized their sexual behaviour.

Indeed, our ability to walk perfectly on two feet obscured signs of the oestrus period, which usually indicate the rutting season in females of non-human primates and elicit an instinctive response in males. So the genus *Homo* no longer has any external markers to stimulate sexual activity, and the sexual act is thus freed from biological constraints. Of course, partners can still perceive 'secondary' signs such as alterations in behaviour, slight changes in the acidity and therefore the smell of the skin, swelling of the chest or mouth, etc. It is quite possible that our ancestors were better able to detect these markers than we are. We have cut ourselves off from aspects of our senses by surrounding ourselves with synthetic products that blur our perceptions. We are now quite unable to reconnect with our ancestral intuitions.*

Bipedalism has entailed another important physical modification, which has inspired sculptors and poets down the ages. In his novella, *House of the Sleeping Beauties*, Nobel Laureate Yasunari Kawabata marvels at this anatomical curiosity:

> *Was it not the glory of the human race to have made woman's breasts so beautiful?*

Thanks to our upright position, the mammary glands of *Homo sapiens* have been permanently put on display. The breasts of women of the genus *Homo* then underwent a slow morphological evolution. Today, breasts comprise a large amount of fatty tissue that creates a swollen shape even when the woman is not breastfeeding. This peculiarity is not seen in any other primate and may present an evolutionary advantage. The zoologist Desmond Morris suggests that breasts may have had an erotic power, echoing that of the buttocks which were already attractive to our quadruped ancestors.

---

* Specific experiences in strip-clubs tend to highlight the fact that women are considered more attractive when they are ovulating – at least judging by the increase in their tips during this short period. It seems, therefore, that to a limited extent modern men have retained this kind of fortuitous intuition when it comes to selecting a partner to impregnate.

However, it is still impossible to find an explanation on which all academics can agree today.

The fact remains that, by standing upright, women surrounded themselves with another mystery. As her reproductive state became unclear, Lady Sapiens forced our ancestors to create new social and emotional frameworks to control sexuality. As sexuality was no longer solely related to instinct and was no longer a reaction to a calendar imposed by periods of female fertility, new socially standardized strategies had to be found. In other words, by liberating itself from biology, physical love found itself inextricably linked with pleasure and symbolic representation. What methods did our ancestors use to make their unions fruitful? They may have been prehistoric, but our distant ancestors showed great ingenuity as they introduced new kinds of cultural behaviour into questions of love.

Sexual Behaviour as a Social Factor

Sexuality must have been a quite significant issue in the daily life and ideas of our ancestors. If fertility was harnessed perfectly, it became possible to expand the group and secure its future by creating new families. The blossoming of a new family unit was an adventure in which Lady Sapiens probably played a leading role. Scientists know very little about the organizational intricacies of prehistoric families, but certain rules can still be deduced from the genetic analysis of ancient populations. For example, Évelyne Heyer highlights how genetic studies show that incest must have been banned, since we know that 'in prehistoric times, marriages between close relatives were an exception'.

Genetically speaking, inbreeding can be detrimental to the health of the children born as a result, and it seems that pre-historic humans knew the laws of blood, at least intuitively. It is possible that this empirical finding led to the establishment of prohibitions we still observe today. This is enough to put paid to a well-established misconception that our ancestors lived in a state of social chaos, if not debauchery, which often led to aggression between groups. As a rule, hunter-gatherer societies have a vested interest in maintaining a peaceful way of life, both inside and outside their group.

Nevertheless, in nineteenth-century Academic art, painters took mischievous pleasure in portraying prehistoric man as a beast unable to contain his aggressive impulses and who spent his time hunting either wild animals or females. One of the clichés most frequently used by exponents of *l'art pompier* was 'wife-capture'.

Paul Jamin's famous painting *A Rape in the Stone Age* is an excellent illustration of Cro-Magnon man's alleged inability to control his impulses, depicting him stealing from a fellow Cro-Magnon a woman with red hair, a symbol of untamed sensuality in the late nineteenth century. For art historian Élisabeth Couturier, this painting is above all a way 'of showing off the body of a desirable woman from every angle'. This fashionable theme provides a pretext for rendering male fantasies in the guise of official art.

Indeed, these scenes depicting contorted bodies highlight the perfection of totally naked female forms. Wife-capture as a genre scene helped inveigle sexuality into bourgeois living rooms, hidden behind the historical subject of the scene.

However, wife-capture probably doesn't correspond to any kind of anthropological reality. For Marylène Patou-Mathis, it 'is one of the great myths that we have allowed to linger for too long. But it is not archaeologically provable, and it has become ingrained in our ideas only through the powerful ancient myth of the abduction of women.'

The anthropologist Michèle Coquet concedes, however, that wife-capture was a possible alternative way of introducing a new gene pool into a group:

Wife-capture exists within populations of hunter-gatherers... but it is not as common as nineteenth-century art pompier would suggest. [And to clarify], wife-capture has been reported in Amazonian regions among Yanomani tribes (who are hunter-gatherers and horticulturalists) when one group attacks another... But such raids happen only occasionally and are not about abducting women – they are often revenge for other conflicts.

If the birth rate was endangered, this might also motivate the practice of wife-capture. For example, 'the ethnologist Pierre Clastres has observed cases of wife-capture among the Guyaki because of a lack of women', continues Michèle Coquet. This motive for wife-capture, which does not promote good neighbourly relations, is linked to economic problems. We know that 'among the Inuit, women are abducted when it's impossible to pay a dowry'.

If wife-capture existed, it was not the dominant practice. Hunter-gatherers probably invented marriage, which is much more advantageous in the long term when it comes to establishing lasting alliances with neighbouring tribes:

Most instances when women were exchanged were through marriage, not wife-capture. Marriage is the most beneficial because it gives access to the resources of other groups. Hunter-gatherers did not move completely freely within an infinite area... Each group 'owned' its territory, and such alliances allowed groups to hunt and gather in neighbouring areas.

Depending on the context, more violent kinds of behaviour might of course have occurred. But scientists agree that a peaceful exchange of women in prehistory was more likely, rather than violently uprooting women from their families. Marylène Patou-Mathis also emphasizes that the term 'exchange' is not disparaging. Indeed, 'anthropological work by Lévi-Strauss sees the exchange of women as a way of creating links between groups, of forging alliances and therefore reducing violence. And such exchanges did not necessarily imply that the woman didn't have a choice of partner.'

Obviously, we should not hope to find an exclusive model that applied to ancient matrimonial strategies on all continents. On the other hand, we can state that the relationships were carefully chosen and concluded according to group-specific rules and that marital anarchy had no part to play.

When we try to imagine what prehistoric relationships were like, another question comes up regularly: were our ancestors monogamous or polygamous? Romain Pigeaud, doctor of prehistoric archaeology, urges us to remain open-minded when it comes to the kinship structures of our ancestors: 'Regarding monogamy and polygamy, no archaeological evidence exists... and anything might have occurred.'

Our imaginations may well run wild on this subject, so anthropologist Michèle Coquet uses statistics drawn up by ethnographers to shepherd our ideas:

We see few instances of polygamy among hunter-gatherer societies. We know of cases of polyandry in the Amazon, but they are caused by catastrophic situations such as a demographic decline in the numbers of women. [...] Ethnographic studies of hunter-gatherers teach us that the privileged type of relationship is monogamy. This is best suited to a society that wishes to limits its numbers ... On the other hand, such monogamous relationships don't necessarily last for life.

So was Lady Sapiens the head of a blended family? It's possible. Also, would she be expected to live with her husband's family? The question may seem impossible to resolve, but this reckons without the skill of paleogeneticists who are now able to track the movements of mitochondrial DNA, which is transmitted only through the maternal line. It is the analysis of this element that allows Professor Évelyne Heyer to identify the main statistical trends:

In the case of our species, it is women primarily who moved from one group to the next. This is linked to what is called 'patrilocality'. When two people from two different populations get married, it is very often the woman who moves. This has reached a rate of 70% in modern societies. However, in the Paleolithic, data suggests that both men and women were exchanged.

Thus, such transactions between geographically distant human groups seem to have been an effective means of forging long-distance economic and political alliances.

Moreover, as the scientist Jean-Jacques Hublin reminds us, 'the women who move from one group to another ensure the transmission of genes as well as traditions, beliefs and skills'. Marriage exchanges are a source of wealth, as Marylène Patou-Mathis confirms: 'By moving, women shared her culture of origin with her new group. In his way, women encouraged progress, technical improvements, etc.'

We can say that Lady Sapiens and her sisters, by uniting with a partner and giving birth, have contributed to the richness of our genetic and cultural heritage. But can we find out how these encounters took place? Was there a subtle game of seduction?

Relationship Rituals between Men and Women

For archaeologists, it's tricky to identify the more ephemeral arts, and the art of seduction is perhaps the most fleeting of all, as it leaves no trace except in the heart of the person being seduced. And fluttering hearts do not turn into fossils, much to the chagrin of prehistorians. In order to imagine the strategies Paleolithic humans used to form relationships, scientists are obliged – once again – to seek the help of ethnology.

When a question cannot be resolved by analysing archaeological sources, cultural anthropology offers a range of interpretations. Such is the case with a question that nagged us throughout our investigation: what might a prehistoric kiss have been like, if it existed? Sheril Kirshenbaum, an American scientist affiliated with Michigan State University and author of the book *The Science of Kissing*, shared the results of her research which she carried out following in the footsteps of the greatest scientists: 'Even Darwin looked at the different traditions and origin of the kinds of behaviour humans use to show affection. So it's a crucial question!'

Kissing is indeed one of the most serious things in life. Whether it's tender as in Klimt's painting, stolen as in Truffaut's movie, a source of oblivion as in Baudelaire's poems or deadly as in Munch's painting *The Kiss of Death*, a kiss is the first gift the person in love desires. This is why Sheril Kirshenbaum cannot imagine a prehistoric world without such a sign of affection:

The general public has an image of prehistoric humans as wild, violent creatures, but for me there's no doubt that they shared gestures of tenderness and took care of each other. Survival is much too difficult without affection: if they hadn't shown affection, we wouldn't be here to talk about it.

The exchange of frequent and elaborate signs of affection is all the more plausible because 'when we look at what is happening in the animal kingdom, and especially with the great apes, we see them hugging and exchanging kisses'.

Why are these gestures so common? For Sheril Kirshenbaum, it's a psychological and social need, but one that's primarily physiological.

Indeed, if we dissect the kiss using the scalpel of molecular biology, it turns out to be an explosive cocktail of dopamine, oxytocin, serotonin and adrenaline. These elements increase the feeling of well-being, but also create a long-term bond between the two partners, thanks in particular to oxytocin, now known as the 'love hormone'. The durability of the bonds between people depends in particular on practical demonstrations of connection. This is why gestures of affection and trust can be shared by relatives, friends or allies. They are not the preserve of lovers, as Sheril Kirshenbaum explains:

Everywhere we look, in history books or in reports by ethnologists who have witnessed displays of affection among so-called 'pre-contact' populations,* we can see how important these exchanges are... And not only between lovers, but also between people who are part of the same family... Especially between mother and child.

While our gestures of affection retain an instinctive element, the manifestations of a close social bond are above all cultural constructs. So to imagine how humans kissed 10,000 BCE, we must give up our modern notions and temporarily forget about kissing on the mouth, and even more so the famous French kiss. An overview of gestures of affection around the world reveals some astonishing practices:

To show affection, people move closer together, hug or rub faces. The gestures can be very varied. In some areas of Canada or among the Maoris, people sniff each other's skin... The only thing that matters is that the two actors share the same codes that allow them to interpret the gesture.

---

* Anthropologists call 'pre-contact societies' those which have not encountered Western civilization and have therefore not yet been influenced by the Western way of life.

Indeed, kissing on the mouth is just one instance in the history of kissing, one note among others in the enormous symphony of the embrace. Popularized in modern times in the West, kissing on the mouth was still misunderstood by many traditional populations until recently. Sheril Kirshenbaum tells us about the misadventures of William Winwood Reade, a British explorer who travelled in Africa in the nineteenth century. On one of his trips, 'he fell in love with the village chief's daughter. But when he finally plucked up the courage to kiss her, she panicked and ran out of the hut. She had never seen this type of behaviour before, and thought he wanted to eat her!'

Kissing on the mouth is thus far from being an anthropological invariant. Admittedly, one day, a monkey gave such a kiss to the famous ethologist Frans de Waal, who was very surprised! But this is not a display commonly seen by primatologists. This gesture does not prove that our ancestors kissed to show their attachment or their desire.

So what might the equivalent of our romantic kiss have been? It can take surprising forms among certain populations, such as the inhabitants of the Trobriand Islands off the east coast of New Guinea. These delicate interpreters of the art of kissing nibble their partner's eyelashes during their most passionate embraces, a discovery that at the time left Bronisław Malinowski, a specialist in 'primitive' sexual behaviour, speechless.

Nevertheless, it is possible some of our ancestors were attracted to the mouth. For Sheril Kirshenbaum, the mouth is a very special contact zone:

Human lips are particularly sensitive, and it's not just a means of expressing affection, but a way of exploring the world – especially when you're a baby. As an adult, we may also remember being fed by adults who pre-chewed food for us.

In addition, women's mouths reveal a lot about their reproductive capacity: 'A rosy and generous mouth is a hormonal barometer for men, who can instinctively recognize that a high level of oestrogen is the cause of such plumpness.'

Finally, Kirshenbaum describes what is commonly called 'genital echo', that is the striking analogy between the lips on the face and those hidden beneath women's clothes.

At present, we know of only one example of a romantic kiss prior to the Neolithic period. On the rock walls of Boqueirão, a site in the prehistoric complex of Pedra Furada in the Brazilian national park of Serra da Capivara, we can see two figures in profile, one smaller than the other, reaching their faces towards each other (see illustration below). While awaiting the future discovery of yet more unambiguous, figurative representations, prehistorians have focused on the other means of attraction that may have existed.

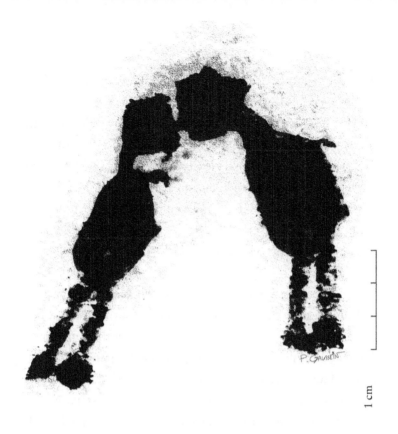

1 cm

A delicate, pre-historic kiss painted in ochre on the rock walls of Boqueirão, a site in the Northeast Region of Brazil, dated 15,000 years BCE according to Niede Guidon, director of the Museo do Homem Americano de São Raimundo, Piauí, Brazil.

To be seductive, you have to stand out from the crowd and be noticed. One universal way of doing this is to show off your talent. Any activity that can prove the physical and cognitive superiority of potential partners can thus become part of the game of seduction.

We need only consider certain finely carved stone tools, such as the wonderful Solutrean laurel-leaf blades, to be convinced that skill was a virtue sought and cultivated by prehistoric people. However, producing the tools necessary for survival did not require a great deal of virtuosity. Common sense and a basic knowledge of the physical properties of lithic raw materials were sufficient to make effective flakes. So why waste time and energy on achieving technical excellence and purity of form? It's likely that the personal pleasure of excelling oneself was the craftsman's primary driving force. The satisfaction of producing a beautiful object may therefore have been the motivation behind the most ornate flint blades. But talent could also be used to attract the attention of potential partners.

To possess another's body without necessarily having to go through a moment of intimacy which is banned anyway in many societies, humans have shown a wealth of ingenuity. The medical doctor and anthropologist Benjamin Brody has studied the strategies used to win the heart of the chosen individual. In the 1980s, in some rural areas of Austria, women performed a dance that amazed the ethnopsychiatrist. The young girls to be married danced with thin slices of apple wedged under their armpits. Their chosen man was then invited to eat the sweat-soaked slices. If he found the taste not unpleasant, then the prospective lovers were allowed get to know each other better.

However absurd it may seem, this example reminds us that the traditions that enable young people to meet each other are diverse. When we try to envision the amorous behaviour of our ancestors, we have to reconnect with our deepest animal nature, and let go of the sad habits engendered by the *Homo technologicus* that we have become. This dance of the apple slices is perfectly ingenious from an evolutionary point of view. Indeed, body odours and tastes are valuable clues to our internal constitution. A drop of sweat can tell us more about a potential lover than any dating-site profile.

During this quest, the behaviour of the chosen partner and their skills are also assessed. This is why dance is one of the most popular weapons of seduction. This subtle art allows its practitioners to show off their psychomotor abilities, their endurance and their sensitivity. And we practice it much more often than we like to imagine, as Michèle Coquet explains:

Among today's hunter-gatherers, dancing is a common practice. It is not only reserved for the grand occasions of collective life (funerals, return from the hunt, initiation). Dance can be part of the games of seduction when it is performed during puberty rites, for example.

This sensuous activity is not the domain of women alone, and when it comes to attracting a partner's attention, men can join in the dance too. Sophie A. de Beaune suggests we should abandon the clichés of the seductive woman and the strong-willed man, citing the example of the Fula people in Africa, where 'it's the men who adorn themselves and dance to seduce the women, while the latter watch. ... It has even been known for a woman to leave her elderly husband, choosing a younger man who seduced her in this way!'

However the dance is organized, there is no reason why prehistoric people would have lacked this means of expression. But how can archaeologists detect evidence of this? Dance can only be surmised through remains that are difficult to interpret, such as artistic representations. Fragments of Magdalenian plaquettes found at the Gönnersdorf and Andernach sites in Germany, two gathering places on either side of the Rhine valley that date back 12,500 years, seem to depict hooded creatures dancing (see illustration page opposite). Romain Pigeaud deciphers these obscure clues handed down to us by our ancestors:

The comma-shaped legs have been identified by Professor Gerhard Bosinski as a representation of dance movements. These are perhaps depictions of marriage dances as we see in ethnography.

And we mustn't forget the plaquette found in La Garenne Cave near Saint-Marcel, Indre, which shows six figures wearing anoraks and holding hands. However, this harmonious line of humans could just as easily be depicting a game-hunting scene as a circular dance to encourage romantic encounters.

Artistic representations aren't the only clues that allow us to detect the existence of dance. Prehistoric musical instruments might also provide indirect proof that people danced, because, as Professor Nicholas Conard rightly points out, 'you can't dance without music. Obviously, there is the possibility of vocalising and clapping your hands... but we can go much further.'

Many types of instruments dating from the Upper Paleolithic have been found. Some are familiar to us, as in the case of the flute, many examples of which have been identified. The three oldest known flutes, two made of swan bone and one of mammoth ivory, were found in the Cave of Geißenklösterle in Germany, and are around 40,000 years old. Other pieces of evidence have been interpreted as potentially more exotic instruments, such as the rhombus, which the musician played by spinning it around on the end of a cord to produce a whirring sound. It is probable that there was an even wider diversity of instruments. The skins used to make drums, the strings and the wooden sound boxes – likely ancestors of harps and guitars – have vanished into the depths of time. And the entire prehistoric orchestra has slipped between the scientists' fingers.

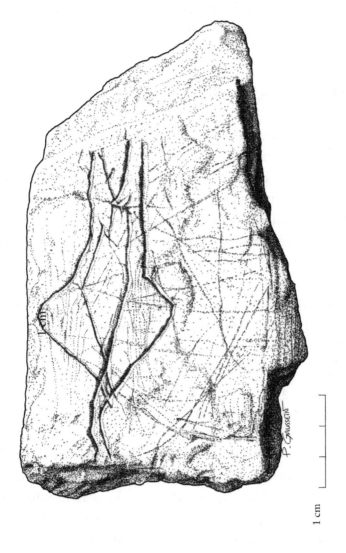

1 cm

On one of the Gönnersdorf plaquettes, two women stand facing each other. They seem to be moving their legs, as if to begin dancing.

Whatever the strategies, seduction is the first step towards another activity that's essential to the survival of the group – sex. Like all intimate practices, however, it remains very difficult to grasp. Nevertheless, some archaeological remains have allowed us to trace the emotions and love-making of our ancestors.

The Clues to Sexuality

Sexuality seems to have played an important role in the daily life and mental universe of prehistoric people, considering the considerable amount of rock art or sculptural depictions that feature human genitalia. The number of elegant Venus figurines with pronounced pubic triangles are legion, and other areas of anatomy with sexual connotations have also been carved onto cave walls.

Indeed, pubic triangles and phalluses have been included discreetly in these pictorial compositions, as part of a more general design. In the Abri de la Madeleine (Madeleine rock shelter) near Tursac, Périgord, for example, these images appear alongside depictions of animals. Randall White, Professor at New York University and Périgord resident by adoption, knows them well:

The Abri Castanet and Abri Blanchard have revealed eight or nine vulvas engraved on the walls. And on one area of wall in the Abri Castanet there are five with two different kinds of shape – one round and another more triangular. This difference raises the question, do the vulvas mean the same thing despite their different shapes?

Some prehistorians interpret these rounded shapes as representations of animal footprints, while others do not rule out the possibility that the artists intended to confuse, even making 'visual puns', such as the 'rod with breasts' found at Dolní Věstonice, which suggests both a Venus and a penis with testicles.

Engraved or painted pubic triangles with pudendal clefts were often accentuated by being located near natural crevices that gave them a full three-dimensional form. Twenty thousand years ago, in a shelter in the Fontainebleau Sandstone region, a tool was used to deepen three wall notches that resembled a vulva, according to scientist Boris Valentin. On the right-hand surface of the wall, a natural crack has been enlarged to resemble a hip and upper thigh. The image overall is strangely reminiscent of Gustave Courbet's *The Origin of the World* (see illustration page 200). In the Chauvet Cave, a bushy pubic triangle framed by two tapering thighs was drawn in charcoal on a stalactite. The pubic area was such an inspiration to prehistoric people that they sometimes made an effort to draw it in places that were difficult to access. As Professor White explains: 'Some vulvas were engraved on the ceiling of the rock shelters. We know this because when we found the engraved surface it was in direct contact with the ground onto which the blocks had collapsed.'

But why is there such a profusion of female sexual representations? Randall White asks the same question: 'Is it a reflection of the respect shown towards women? Is it the expression of a desire to make these images have a positive impact on the daily life of hunter-gatherers?

The questions are very much open-ended, but we have no answers.'

Symbols of female genitalia weren't the only private parts to capture the attention of artists in the past. The male member, although much less common, has sometimes been engraved on cave walls, and some male figures are shown with erections. Full-relief (i.e. three-dimensional) phalluses have been carved on teeth or ivory rods, and a few adorn the end of perforated reindeer antlers. The purpose of these 'perforated batons' is still the subject of debate among experts, the most commonly accepted hypothesis being that they were used to straighten spears made from naturally curving bone or antler. In any case, these rare phallus-shaped specimens – less than ten for every hundred known female figurines – are life-size representations, which has perplexed some scientists. Oscar Fuentes, a prehistorian at the Centre national de la Préhistoire de Périgueux, describes the bold hypotheses of some of his colleagues:

> Marc Martinez and his team have studied penis-shaped objects from the Roc-de-Marcamps site (Gironde, Middle Magdalenian). Anatomical details, such as the penis, are depicted with a high degree of realism. The team's hypothesis is that these batons were used during ceremonies related to sexuality. They even talk about sex toys.

The proliferation of sexual representations created throughout prehistory raises many questions. Are we looking at fertility symbols? Are these tools for performing magic linked to reproduction? Or, more superficially, are they describing sexual practices?

It seems difficult to visualize our ancestors' romantic lives without indulging in fantasy and speculation. But the art on these engraved plaquettes exists nevertheless, almost unnoticed and little-known to the general public, and it provides us with human history's very first *Kama Sutra*. On plaquettes discovered hidden away in the caves in Enlène, Ariège and La Marche, Vienne, curious scenes might be able to shine a light on the sexuality of our ancestors (see illustration page 92). In one instance, two superimposed engraved bodies have been interpreted as representing a couple having sex doggy style, in another two silhouettes suggest a couple, standing up and closely entwined. We should note, however, that scientists are far from being unanimous in their interpretation of these two scenes.

The techniques used to create these works make them difficult to understand. The plaquettes present a jumble of engraved lines that are complex to disentangle. We don't know whether they underwent some kind of process that made them more visible at the time they were made. Nevertheless, today we see an inextricable entanglement of lines drawn one on top of one another in a way that makes it very difficult to understand the various original drawings. How can we be sure that the two women depicted head-to-tail in the La Marche Cave were actually two parts of one composition by the artist? If so, we could be in the presence of the very first representation of oral and homosexual sex in the history of art. Other practices might have been represented: Oscar Fuentes mentions 'an engraved plaquette with a female hand near an erect penis', found at Enlène (see illustration on the following page, bottom left).

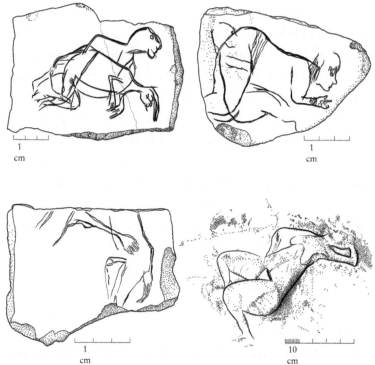

Left-hand column: two plaquettes engraved with sexual scenes found in the Enlène Cave in Ariège. Top right: a depiction found in the Cave of La Marche, Vienne; bottom right: a woman reclining sensuously on the wall of La Magdelaine des Albis Cave, near Penne, Tarn.

Some scientists even believe they can see liquid coming out of the penis. It is therefore possible that we are witnessing a scene of masturbation that is over 10,000 years old. In the face of all this evidence, some scientists were keen to identify this as erotica – even pornography!

For scientists today, it's hard not to see male fantasies reflected in the generous breasts of the Venus figurines and in the pubic areas engraved on the cave walls. However, many prehistorians dismiss this hypothesis as anachronistic. Nicholas Conard's clearly thinks it's 'absurd'.

We must know how to recognize our own contemporary projections... and avoid mapping them directly onto the past. [...] Of course our ancestors had a concept of affection and eroticism. But there is nothing that allows us to argue that this was characterized by male domination, as is the case in the contemporary notion of pornography. In any case, that's not what I see in the Venus of Hohle Fels.

When shown the headlines in certain magazines that describe prehistoric humans as sexually obsessed, Catherine Schwab laughs, reminding us that 'The proportion of sexual representations found in Paleolithic art is no greater than in other periods of art history'. And she points to the many depictions of phalluses in the Roman era and the lascivious paintings of the Renaissance.

Professor Denis Vialou emphasizes the changing nature of sexual practices from the past up until today: 'Sexuality is the ultimate social construct, based on many different norms that ultimately intersect. [...] Eroticism is completely different from one society to another. There is no one norm.'

When asked whether prehistoric humans might have been fixated with copulation, Nicholas Conard puts things in perspective:

Were Paleolithic people obsessed with sex? No, no more than we are. But it is a factor that's essential to the survival of the group. You can sing, dance, do a million things, but nothing is as essential for a population to thrive as successful reproduction.

So it's possible that the quest for sexual pleasure was at the heart of our ancestors' personal concerns, because such positive exchanges strengthened the links between individuals – as well as ensuring more pregnancies.

And this raises another issue: did prehistoric humans make the link between sexuality and procreation? One exceptional archaeological site seems to provide some answers to this crucial question.

Sexuality and Procreation

Our investigation in search of prehistoric women continues in the Roc-aux-Sorciers rock shelter in Vienne. This archaeological site was discovered in 1927 by Lucien Rousseau, and is famous for its impressive sculpted frieze depicting, among other things, some amazing life-size women. These limestone Venus figures were discovered in 1950 – appropriately by two women. Suzanne de Saint-Mathurin and Dorothy Garrod had no idea that their discovery would be classified as an historic monument on 18 January 1955.

The Roc-aux-Sorciers rock shelter enjoys the kind of ideal position that humans particularly liked to inhabit. The site's scientific director, Geneviève Pinçon tells us: '15,000 years ago, at Roc-aux-Sorciers, there was a cliff facing due south with a magnificent view over the valley and the River Anglin, as well as crossing points where the animals would congregate'.

The location was inhabited during the Upper Paleolithic, and some 15,000 years ago it was a place where artists displayed their talents. This point is important because it is a rare and valuable thing to be able to date prehistoric works of art. Indeed, archaeologists are often faced with problems of chronology because engravings do not contain materials that can be dated using methods such as carbon-14 dating. Roc-aux-Sorciers is an exceptional case: amid the archaeological sediment, prehistorians were lucky enough to discover fragments of works that had become detached when the wall collapsed. The sculpted wall could thus be dated by association with the fragments of frieze found in the surface occupation site. What is more, this site is also remarkable for the monumentality of its works. The surface of the ceiling alone comprises 500 m^2 of decorations, but, as Geneviève Pinçon tells us, 'the fresco probably covers an area twice as large as we have been able to uncover. An area just 20 metres in length has been exposed, and another 20 metres have been protected as an archaeological reserve.'

It's enough to provide some amazing discoveries in the years to come, by which time our technologies will be able to offer new kinds of analysis. The artworks in this rock shelter must be contemplated in silence, as their craftsmanship is masterful and their size imposing: 'These are monumental sculptures, depicting life-size human and animal figures. These works were visible from afar because the landscape at the time was open tundra.'

Two male ibex (top) seem to be fighting over the favours of a female on heat (bottom left), with her kid (bottom right). Engravings on the wall of the Roc-aux-Sorciers rock shelter, Vienne.

On the panel of rock wall we can see today, two ibex and possibly a male human head welcome the visitor. Then comes a herd of goats with two rutting males (above) who are fighting over the favours of the female on heat with her kid (below); a few steps further on, the wonderful triptych of women is followed by a scene of horses, and finally two bison bring this astonishing 15-metre frieze to an end.

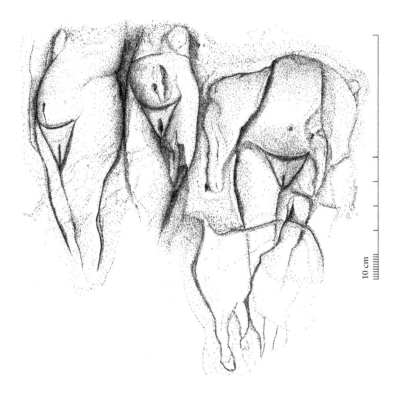

10 cm

Three almost life-size nude women, possibly depictions
of the 'three ages of life' appear on the wall of the
Roc-aux-Sorciers rock shelter, Vienne.

These delicate works required some initial preparation
of the rock wall, which was smoothed down before the work of
engraving began. If we as modern observers mainly see deep
furrows on a solid cream-coloured background, our perception
is undoubtedly incomplete. Just as medieval cathedrals were
polychrome, it's quite possible that the engravings
were enhanced using colours. Indeed, Geneviève Pinçon was
thrilled to detect traces of pigment: 'A figure was sculpted,
engraved and then painted.'

The models are particularly realistic. This characteristic is not unique in prehistoric art, and there are many such figures, such as the horses at Chauvet and the bisons at Altamira in Spain. However, at Roc-aux-Sorciers, the artist showed real originality in their treatment of the anthropomorphic figure. Geneviève Pinçon's enthusiasm for the images is infectious: 'Such well-characterized human figures whose faces are depicted in ana-tomical detail are unparalleled anywhere else in the world!'

Standing proudly in front of the panel of women, she describes the treasure of which she is the keeper:

First we have a woman face-on, then a woman in pro-file who bears the linea nigra found on young pregnant women... And then there's a third woman, who is not at all curvaceous: she is probably a young girl or a very old woman. This panel is unique. We have three life-size women without heads, feet or arms.

Emphasis has been placed on signs of femininity, as with most female figurines. 'The irregularities on the surface of the wall have been used to emphasize the vulva of the first woman. We can also see the detail of her nipple.' Here, indi-viduality is outweighed by anatomical detail.

For Geneviève Pinçon this means that that the artists' discourse goes way beyond a realistic representation of the women in their group: 'We are looking at the complete cycle of a woman's life represented generically. It's the story of a body that is fertile at a certain point, and no longer fertile at other times.'

So is this monumental fresco really an ode to fertility? For Catherine Schwab, there is little doubt: 'It's a representation of the young girl, the woman who has just given birth, but also probably the post-menopausal woman. We have a representation of the three stages of life, which still revolves around the experience of childbirth.'

Supporting this interpretation, Oscar Fuentes finds a symbolic echo in some details of the animal pictures at the site: 'The "motherhood" aspect of the female bison is very important because it has been given anatomical details that are not normally present, like an udder and udder teats.' The ibex panel also offers a summary of the behaviour of these animals in rut, as well as a possible allegory of fertility:

This is probably a confrontation between two males in rut and, below, the female who is lifting her tail to show her dilated vulva. She is also accompanied by one of her young. The message is pretty clear. The feminine character of this female ibex is also highlighted by the under-engraving of the lower part of a woman's body.*

For Oscar Fuentes, the discourse is crystal clear: 'At Roc-aux-Sorciers, the artists are clearly pursuing a common theme of fertility.'

According to Geneviève Pinçon, the tribe at Roc-aux-Sorciers was probably carving a kind of educational frieze in the rock, like a comic strip, to explain the link between the sexual act and procreation. 'The Magdalenians were men and women like us: they understood everything. The ibex

---

* The frieze was not created in one go. Scientists have established three separate periods of creation, probably corresponding to three seasons of occupancy. This explains why some engravings were made on top of others. For the scientists, this visual 'layer cake' strengthens the symbolism of the sculpted images.

panel illustrates this unambiguously; we see the female, her kid and the rutting males.' Pinçon is sure that our ancestors understood completely the stages of human and animal reproduction.

The connection is obvious. In addition, this panel echoes the one depicting three women in the three ages of life, which itself takes a more conceptual if not mythological approach.

While some people still believe – unlike the vast majority of prehistorians – that Lady Sapiens's contemporaries did not understand the cycle of life, for Nicholas Conard, there is no possible doubt:

Some people argue that prehistoric humans did not understand reproduction. I personally think that is highly unlikely. These people were much more connected to their environment than we are. You don't have to be a genius to understand that, like all other animals, when you have sex, you get pregnant.

Geneviève Pinçon adds: 'There's a link between the women and the bison. Perhaps it's highly symbolic, because the bison is one of the few mammals whose gestation period is the same as that of humans, lasting nine months.' In this way, the local inhabitants proved that they had a perfect understanding of the processes of procreation.

'All these elements tend to show that this site is the product of a complex intellectual and symbolic narrative. But what is the discourse hidden behind this astonishing fresco? It's difficult to give a definitive interpretation. In any case, it seems highly unlikely that this was the representation of a banal scene of everyday life as the involvement of the population in carrying out the work was so great.' For Geneviève Pinçon, 'they may have wanted to depict a myth... or a fact of nature, or a concept...'.

For Oscar Fuentes, this is a personalization of ancestral knowledge in a way that can be understood by as many people as possible: 'This panel does not depict women, but rather an allegory of fertility. [...] All this brings us back to a kind of symbolic thinking that links humans and animals.'

It is also possible that prehistoric people developed a mythology around human fertility, relating it to the environment and to animals. Indeed, in traditional societies the sexual act is rarely seen as a simple operation consisting of the 'clinical' creation of new life. Michèle Coquet explains this anthropological invariant:

We know that a sexual act between a man and a woman is necessary to conceive a child. But it's never enough. Indigenous theories of reproduction are sometimes very complex.

In the creation of a new human being, magic and spirituality permeate cosmogonic tales and narratives:

External beings (spirits of the dead, forces of nature) also contribute to the emergence of the new human being. For Indigenous Australians, the man opens up the path for the new child through the sexual act, then nourishes it with his sperm. The woman goes looking for babies in sacred places in order to conjure them up in her womb. This kind of walk is recommended during the woman's menstruation.

It's quite possible that prehistoric people performed this kind of discourse and invented gestures intended to promote human reproduction. Creating a family is a universal adventure that has concerned women since the dawn of humanity.

Chapter 5

STARTING A FAMILY

When trying to imagine the personal life of prehistoric women, it's essential to find out about their families. What was the family structure? How was daily life organized? How were mothers able to go about their activities despite having to look after nursing babies and bring up older children?

Through fascinating interviews with specialists in paleo-genetics, primatology and anthropology we've been able to produce portraits of these early families. All the scientists agree that the figurehead of the family unit was always the mother, and her life was to be protected at all costs. Teacher and scientist Nicholas Conard stresses that, in anthropological terms, this goes without saying:

It's crucial for the group's demographics that women remain healthy. Losing a man is undesirable, but it's not that bad. By contrast, if the women and children start dying, the situation becomes very tricky.

In the Paleolithic period, there were many causes of death, in particular during childbirth, which was considered a precarious time before the invention of modern medicine. Indeed, over a period of 7 million years, the evolution of bipedalism restructured the female pelvis and modified the mechanics of childbirth. In addition, the volume of the skull in the genus *Homo* increased during our evolution. But are these changes in themselves obstacles to childbirth? Would these limitations increase the risk of mother and child dying during labour?

Getting Ahead

The hominini who lived 2 million years ago had brains that were 20% larger than the great apes. But their brains were still between three and four times smaller than that of today's humans.

Jean-Jacques Hublin, director of the Department of Human Evolution at the Max Planck Institute in Leipzig and a world-renowned expert, holds up skull casts as he explains. Unfortunately, no fossilized brains dating from the time of Lady Sapiens have been found. But scientists have been able to make advances by analysing skulls, as they bear indirect witness to the functioning of the brain, an organ that's essential to understanding our evolution. Scientists were thus able to establish the extent to which our brain and skull evolved rapidly in the genus *Homo*.

To enable brain size to increase without raising the risk of maternal death during childbirth, evolution has provided us with a strategy hidden within our skeleton. The infant skull is unusually small by comparison with the size of the adult human skull, and this 'disproportion is much greater in humans than in other apes', notes Professor Hublin. And, holding up another cast, he highlights another uniquely human feature:

Here is the skull of a seven-day-old newborn baby – it's tiny. Between birth and adulthood the size of the brain increases fourfold. At birth, the brain is only 23% of its mature size, whereas chimpanzees, when they are born, have a brain measuring almost 40% of its ultimate size. And for macaques, it's as big as 70%.

Indeed, a human child is born with a small brain and its growth takes place mainly outside the mother's uterus, only reaching adult size at the age of around fourteen or fifteen.

Growth of this magnitude outside the womb is uniquely human. It enables the development of a larger adult head size than in any other primate and means that childbirth is always possible. Of course, the size of the brain is not the end of the story in the evolution of human behaviour:

It's not just the size of the brain that changes, but also its organization. Around 300,000 years ago we reached an average brain capacity of 1,400 cm³ – today's adult size. Specifically in the lineages that lead to today's modern humans (sapiens), *we can see that the cranium becomes much more globular. This change goes hand in hand with a reorganization of the brain, especially in the cerebellum which, we believe, is involved in the production of language, in social interactions and their reward circuit.*

These factors have led human beings to become what fully defines them today: a special kind of ape, capable of creating symbols and concepts, of having abstract thoughts, of making tools and machines, of forging connections and networks of exchange with their fellow human beings. These cerebral characteristics also make us highly social animals. They constitute the fertile ground that gave rise to agrarian societies, to civilizations and, today, to the growth of our highly connected society. Our evolution has been ongoing since prehistoric times, and, as Professor Hublin points out, it will only stop with the extinction of our species. And so, 'over the last 10,000 years, we have seen a slight reduction in the size of the brain in *sapiens*'. This reduction is linked to the fact that brain volume is proportionate to height, and in the European Upper Paleolithic, *Homo sapiens* was very tall, with an average male height of 1.80 metres.

Giving Birth – Not Such a Risky Business

Bipedalism is a core feature of the hominid family of which we are members. Experts are still speculating about which of our most distant ancestors stood on his hind legs on a regular basis. Among the favourite candidates are *Sahelanthropus tchadensis* known as Toumaï and discovered in Chad (7 million years old), *Orrorin tugenensis* found in Kenya (6 million years old) and Ethiopian *Ardipithecus ramidus* (4.4 million years old). It is very difficult to decide between these pretenders to the throne of the first biped, the first to have defied the laws of gravity. Beyond divergences of expert opinion, 3.6 million-year-old footprints found in Tanzania prove beyond doubt that walking is an age-old legacy. Thanks to these millennia of walking upright, Lady Sapiens, who lived in the Upper Paleolithic, was therefore completely bipedal.

Standing upright revolutionized our bodies and our behaviour both as individuals and in terms of society as a whole. However, women's lives were transformed even more because this genuinely revolutionary change in posture modified their pelvis in a quite considerable way. July Bouhallier, doctor of human paleontology and director of the Institut de Recherche et d'Actions pour la Santé des Femmes (Institute for Research and Action on Women's Health), describes this transformation:

The practice of bipedalism completely rearranged the pelvis. It went from an extended shape that is specific to non-human primates, to a shape that is said to be 'under pressure', i.e. that is shorter and wider to help support the upright position.

This modification to the pelvis obviously affects both sexes in our species. However, unlike the male pelvis, the female pelvis is not just a tool for walking and a bowl-shaped cup for holding in our intestines. Women also use it to carry babies and give birth, and so they have had to deal with new challenges during childbirth: 'The bottom of the spine closes off the pelvis, which forces the foetus to bend to pass through the gap. So this alters the way the foetus moves within the pelvic cavity to exit the mother's womb.'

But Lady Sapiens was quite able to overcome these natural modifications resulting from evolution. The female body as well as that of the baby developed various solutions allowing the latter to find its way through the birth canal, despite this considerable morphological transformation. First, the baby's bones, in particular those in its head, are not yet knitted together. In fact, the skull comprises several movable bony plates and the fontanelles, those 'spaces between the bones of an infant's skull which allow the different sections of the skull to overlap as the baby is delivered through a narrow birth canal'.

This ingenious natural stratagem goes hand in hand with another important phenomenon:

Women in labour produce large quantities of relaxin, a hormone that makes the joints more flexible. This softens the pelvis so that the various pelvic bones move apart to adapt to the size of the child and facilitate its journey.

During childbirth, the expectant mother may also perform a series of highly intuitive gestures. For example, undulating movements in the pelvis reinforce the effect of the relaxin to 'loosen' the pelvic bones as well as speed up the dilation of the cervix. But to enable such freedom of movement, the recumbent position, now adopted almost systematically in Western hospitals, is not the best. For July Bouhallier, it seems unnatural, as she explains:

The recumbent position developed at the same time as hospitalized childbirth became the norm. [...] However, vertical positions are much more efficient. They allow the pelvis to become more mobile and in particular the sacrum, which cannot move if it is impeded by the delivery table.

There are lots of positive aspects to a standing position, going well beyond mere freedom of movement: 'You can make the most of gravity, it prevents a lot of pain for the mother and it allows her to breathe more easily.'

Staying in an upright position is therefore more natural, as traditional practices make clear. Equally, in many societies, women give birth in a squatting position. It would never occur to today's women hunter-gatherers to lie on their back to give birth, and our ancestors – both recent and distant – must have used this technique which seems to be common sense:

When we look back at early depictions of childbirth, since antiquity women have always adopted an upright position. Whether they are kneeling, squatting or standing, their bodies are always vertical.

This position even allows the mother to maintain her independence and give birth without the aid of midwives, 'like the women of the San people in the Kalahari, who give birth alone in the desert', as anthropologist Michèle Coquet reminds us.

For a successful birth, the experience and instinct of the mother must have been decisive. However, within a community as close-knit and united as that of prehistoric humans, it is of course possible to imagine that women intervened to help the woman giving birth in the event of problems. It is very likely that techniques to aid delivery spread among the female population through personal experience. Nicholas Conard thinks that the Venus figurines may have played a role in the transmission of women's knowledge about fertility. When describing the Venus of Hohle Fels, Conard sees her as more than just an object – she was most certainly a mediator of practical and symbolic debates within the Paleolithic community of women:

Knowledge associated with human reproduction and child-birth, as well as many other aspects of fertility in the broadest sense, could be transmitted from generation to generation using this object.

Nevertheless, we can't verify this hypothesis of the 'paleo-midwife'. On the other hand, the study of evolution teaches us that the female anatomy is certainly highly adapted to the act of giving birth without major obstacles. As July Bouhallier observes: 'We have seen no pelvic morphology that would indicate a risk of maternal death. In other words, the pelvis wasn't shaped in a way that could impede childbirth, other than in cases of disease.'

If that hadn't been the case, we wouldn't be here discussing all this today.

Mother of Many?

According to cultural anthropologist Michèle Coquet, women did not have to wait for modern birth control in order to understand their bodies, citing a perfect knowledge of how to regulate pregnancies among the populations she has studied:

Women know very well that as soon as their periods stop, that means they are carrying a child. They understand their menstrual cycle and their fertility. They also practice abstinence when they don't want to get pregnant.

For Dr Coquet, 'women are mistresses of their own fertility. They know about plants that will induce abortion allowing them to manage their childbearing as they wish.'

Given our ancestors' empirical knowledge of the plant world, this kind of plant was certainly consumed during prehistory, and is a practice that has continued over the centuries. For example, in antiquity, Plutarch points out that by observing the behaviour of goats women came to understand that eating dictamus (also known as dittany of Crete), a herb related to oregano, induced early miscarriage of a foetus. So mothers would likely have imitated wild goats as a way of getting rid of burdensome pregnancies. Soranos of Ephesus also describes various methods that can be used during the first thirty days of pregnancy in order to abort an unborn child. Some suggestions are amusing, such as jumping up and down or drinking a glass of light wine. Others might end up being effective because they are physiologically traumatic, such as 'getting tossed around in a cart' or 'purging with a douche'. Introducing warm, sweetened oil into the vagina is also suggested as an effective method of abortion.

Few doctors in antiquity protested against abortion, but they agreed on the fact that earlier interventions are preferable for the health of the mother-to-be – preventing fertilization from taking place remaining the ideal solution. The ancient Egyptians knew about intravaginal products: these thick, paste-like concoctions probably served to block the birth canal at least in part, and with it the progress of sperm.

Despite all these precautions, unwanted pregnancies would of course sometimes occur. Michèle Coquet explains that, if the pregnancy could not be avoided or cut short, women in traditional societies may have resorted to infanticide:

The San women of the Kalahari give birth alone in the desert and decide on their own whether the baby they have just given birth to will live or die. That does not mean that it's an easy decision, even if their choice is also clearly made in light of living conditions within the group.

Despite all the birth control strategies available to her, did Lady Sapiens decide to have a large family? Nineteenth-century academic painting or *l'art pompier*, notably through works such as Léon Maxime Faivre's *Two Mothers*, created an indelible image of a prehistoric woman surrounded by lots of children clinging to her breasts. But is this a distorted view? Were large families desirable – and above all manageable – for Upper Paleolithic hunter-gatherers?

Our ancestors' way of life was not conducive to having lots of offspring, as they had to face numerous physical constraints. First of all, daily work involved short to medium-length journeys. But above all, a significant degree of mobility was necessary during the seasonal migrations between different encampments. Michèle Coquet also reminds us that, among today's hunter-gatherers, 'pregnancies happen every four to five years. Their demanding lifestyle requires births to be regulated.'

Equally Jean-Jacques Hublin finds it 'unrealistic to imagine large families. Women's fertility is generally lower in the Paleolithic than in the Neolithic period.'

Having a child is not just a question of biology and environment. It's a decision that results from both personal and cultural choices. So how many children did Lady Sapiens choose to have in her family? Even just a few years ago, it would have been very ambitious to hope for an answer. But advances in science and the development of new fields of investigation now make it possible to overcome this silence. This is in particular thanks to research carried out by Vincent Balter, a CNRS research director affiliated to Lyon's École Normale Supérieure.

Discoveries about Breastfeeding and Weaning

Vincent Balter is a specialist in calcium isotopes and it was through such analysis that he was able to determine the weaning age of Australopithecus and *Homo erectus* children, which may shed light on the periods that followed.

Every object – a blade of grass, a piece of meat or a drop of water – made up of carbon, hydrogen and a host of other chemical elements, contains a very specific signature according to its isotopic composition. So each piece of food ingested by an animal or a person will leave its isotopic signature behind, marking them in a way in their flesh, bones and teeth. And it's possible to detect these elements long after an individual's death. Carbon, strontium and calcium are particularly interesting: the first allows us to date an individual's skeletal remains (this is the famous carbon 14), the second, their geographical origin, and the third, how long they were breastfed for in early childhood.

Since teeth record calcium levels as they grow, these levels can be measured by taking micro-samples from the crown of a tooth from top to bottom to monitor its growth. Vincent Balter can thus identify the weaning period, when the child gives up breast milk and adopts a more varied diet.

Breast milk also has specific features that make the breast-feeding period very apparent when studying the dentin of teeth. Vincent Balter has unlocked these secrets:

The calcium isotopes in breast milk have a very particular and unique signature. Measuring maternal calcium levels in different areas of the tooth, that is at different ages of its growth, allows us to collect data on the weaning age.

The result tends to show that the duration of breastfeeding was relatively long, compatible with what is practiced in non-industrialized populations. Vincent Balter believes that this human behaviour is ancient:

In the case of Homo erectus *2 million years ago, we found the characteristic signatures of milk until the age of four, which shows that small children were nursed for a long time by their parents. Between 2 million years ago and the Upper Paleolithic, it is unlikely that the child's needs were any less.*

To conduct his investigation, Balter carried out his isotopic studies on the milk teeth of *Australopithecus* (3 million years old), *Paranthropus*, (two species related to but more robust than *Australopithecus*; 3 million years old), *Homo erectus* (2 million years old), today's apes and modern humans.

Additional analyses will soon be carried out on teeth from the Upper Paleolithic (40,000 to 10,000 years ago). The scientific adventure has only just begun to investigate these trails. However, it is unlikely that Lady Sapiens's breastfeeding was very different from what has been observed in the case of *Homo erectus*. On the contrary, Vincent Balter believes that it is 'reasonable to assume that this pattern remained constant during the period when the brain continued to grow'.

Weaning baby *sapiens*, at around three or four years old, nevertheless occurred earlier than in the case of our cousins the great apes, who nurse their young until they are eight years old but in a very different way. Indeed, small gorillas, chimpanzees and orangutans, to name just a few, learn to feed on their own very quickly, but without abandoning the mother's breast which they suckle from time to time. Food diversification thus occurs very early on in these species.

Experts were not surprised by the results of this study, because a long period of breastfeeding brings many benefits to traditional populations. First and foremost, milk offers baby *sapiens* a healthy and rich diet. Second, breastfeeding inhibits fertility and mimics the effects of modern chemical contraception. Since women rarely get pregnant while they are producing milk, extended breastfeeding is an additional birth-control device.

As mothers usually do not conceive while breastfeeding, knowing the weaning age helps to estimate the time between each pregnancy. By means of a simple calculation, Vincent Balter can therefore be sure that women certainly did not have very large families:

> *As Paleolithic women were able to bear children until they were about thirty, if we say breastfeeding went on for two or three years, and they gave birth to their first child at around fourteen, that gives us a maximum of five or six births per woman.*

This is a reasonable average, not counting the high mortality rate among young children. It enabled Lady Sapiens and her peers to bring up their children in comfortable conditions, especially as the children would be raised and nurtured by the whole group – a finding of Jean-Jacques Hublin, working with the American sociobiologist Sarah Blaffer Hrdy, a pioneer of evolutionary psychology.

Humans and 'Cooperative Reproduction'

The fact that part of the brain's growth takes place after birth is very important for the child's development, when the newborn and the infant start to perceive the outside world and interact with members of their group. As the brain matures in a social environment, this increases and develops the cognitive capacities of these small humans, who show enormous potential for taking advantage of their environment during their childhood. 'There's dad, mum, the dog, people are talking all around you. There are all kinds of stimuli that will influence the establishment of cerebral networks,' explains Jean-Jacques Hublin.

It is during this stage of life, up to the age of five or six, that many social stimuli take place, and it is also now that the child needs their loved ones' undivided attention. In order to get help from their mother, the child can rely on a hormone that's had a lot of publicity in recent years – oxytocin. 'As they are giving birth and immediately afterwards, mothers are awash with oxytocin: it's a hormone that promotes attachment behaviour.'

Physical proximity to the mother – reinforced by breast-feeding – facilitates the emergence of a kind of love that will become even more symbiotic as the baby sends strong signals to their mother to show their desire for contact. It's not just about getting cuddles, which promote the development of feelings of affection, but also and above all because their survival is at stake. The baby is far from autonomous when it comes to feeding themselves, and they will play all their trump cards to get fed, using a whole arsenal of facial expressions and showing a very special ability to decode what is called 'non-verbal communication'.

Even after weaning, the child remains dependent on the group. This is why they must learn to attract the attention of others and quickly understand the intentions of the individuals surrounding them.

To nurture this communication, the child begins by imitating the individuals in their group. They pay special attention to the faces of relatives and, despite their fuzzy eyesight, they are able to recognize their mother's face from the age of two months.

Indeed, children are consummate observers: ethologists and psychologists have found out that young children focus much more than young apes do on the behaviour of other members of their group. Moreover, reading the emotions of adults is easier in humans than in animals. 'The whites of human eyes are very big,' Jean-Jacques Hublin explains, 'which makes it easy to see the direction of our gaze, while monkeys' eyes have no white areas so it is their head movements that are noticed.'

Relying on eye movements makes it possible to read the sometimes hidden intentions of our peers in a much more subtle way. Such a superior understanding of other people's ulterior motives leads to faster socialization and promotes interaction with the group. For children, these interactions are based on a desire rarely seen in monkeys (except in marmosets) – that of pleasing others. For the child, stimulating a positive feeling in adults is a question of survival, while 'in other great apes, once the baby is weaned, it can feed on its own,' explains the American anthropologist Kristen Hawkes. 'This is not the case with humans. Even when they are weaned, children are dependent on those around them.'

So baby *sapiens* appeals to emotions, then displays altruistic behaviour as soon as they are old enough to understand that this is valued by the community: for example, sociologists have noticed that children are very willing to share their food with others. Even tiny children understand the fundamental importance of sharing to create a lasting bond of trust.

To bring the *sapiens* child up successfully, the group's help is of course welcome and, here again, evolution benefits small humans by widening attachment to include a broad group around them and not just their mother.

Humans are one of the rare species to engage in 'cooperative reproduction'. This highly unromantic term signifies an investment by the parents and the whole group in the upbringing of their offspring. For *Homo sapiens*, Jean-Jacques Hublin explains, 'raising a child to adulthood is no longer the sole responsibility of the mother, it's a collective project that involves several members of the group.'

In the animal kingdom, other species share our way of going about things: hyenas and some primates also engage in cooperative reproduction. But this kind of organization is far from being predominant in the animal kingdom, and no other species has developed this system as extensively as we have.

To maximize the chances of the offspring's survival, the group helped the mother during the first months of breast-feeding, protecting her, but also giving her partial or total nutritional support during her newborn's first few months of life. Some scientists estimate that this kind of care for children and their mothers began 1.8 million years ago with *Homo erectus*.

From a certain age, all other members of the group could feed the child using pre-mastication, which ethnologists have observed in present-day hunter-gatherer tribes.

Childcare is also a service that different members of the community can provide. This behaviour can also be seen in some monkeys, for example in mother chimpanzees, who share the care of their young. And just like humans, they require reliable references. In ape populations, such 'nannies' are considered to be all the more useful if they have already experienced motherhood themselves.

But we shouldn't think that the protective instinct is a female preserve. Following the example of some male chimpanzees who adopt orphans, men are capable of devoting themselves not only to their own children, but also to children outside their close family circle. Why they do this can also be found in the attachment hormone:

It's not just women who produce oxytocin. Men also secrete it. We can see its influence on fathers, grandfathers... and grandmothers, of course!

And talking about these close relatives, it's time to mention one of the very first quiet transformations in our history – 'the granny revolution'.

Grandmothers Go Down in History

Seeing them working in the sun for hours and hours, harvesting plants, doing all this highly physical activity, I realized how hard their work was. And looking in depth at the temporal data, I found that they were doing more than everyone else in the group.

It all started when Kristen Hawkes, Emerita Professor at the University of Utah, was observing the activities of the Hadza people in Tanzania, and her attention was particularly drawn to post-menopausal women.

With her colleague Sarah Hrdy, Kristen Hawkes chose to describe these women as 'grandmothers'. This term refers to the category of women who have already given birth but are no longer able to do so. It's a very important population both socially and in terms of numbers. Indeed, 'we just have to look at the age structure in modern human groups – a third of the women in the population are no longer fertile.'

This may be the case for modern humans, but were there many grandmothers in the Upper Paleolithic? Kristen Hawkes suggests looking again at our traditional notions of life expectancy to construct a more realistic vision of the past:

When we look at life expectancy in ancient populations, we get the impression that people died young. But we mustn't forget that this is a mathematical calculation aimed at establishing an average that's strongly influenced by the high number of infant deaths and the accidental deaths of men whose activities were dangerous. These deaths greatly reduce the estimate of life expectancy, but in reality there were lots of grandmothers in prehistory, as certain burials show. People did not necessarily die early and there were many post-menopausal women in the population.

Sophie A. de Beaune clarifies this nuance in demographic statistics:

What varied was the probability of reaching old age, which was much lower than today, but, once they had got beyond infancy and childbearing age for women, people could be optimistic about living to an advanced age. By the time they reached adulthood, a healthy man or woman could expect to live sixty years.

Indeed, menopause is not a phenomenon of post-industrial societies, as we are sometimes told. Women experience menopause in non-industrialized societies, and there is no reason they didn't go through it in prehistoric times too. For Kristen Hawkes, the menopause, which is known only in mammals and which women share only with certain species of cetacean, helps to explain our increased longevity.

We then asked why our childbearing period is so short? Why do women survive for so long after their childbearing functions have stopped?

The answer focuses on the value of mature women: it's because post-menopausal women have a vital role to play in the survival of the youngest members of the group. The end of fertility long before death is clearly an evolutionary benefit. A woman with one or more decades of life ahead of her but who can no longer bear children will be able to invest her energy in the survival of her own children and grandchildren.

Even after they're weaned, children must rely on those around them for food. They are dependent on their mother initially, until she has another child. Then it's the post-menopausal women who become the providers of food for their daughter's children. Or their daughter-in-law's – that works too! Relying on the help of grandmothers therefore allows a woman to have children more frequently, because she knows that her most recent child will be taken care of by the older women.

By providing assistance to a woman of reproductive age, making her calmer and more productive, grandmothers ensured the perpetuation of their own genes. It is much more advantageous to create a line of reproducing woman who support each other than to go through several pregnancies alone, risking death and leaving in the care of the group a child who's too young to be independent.

Our study shows that females who survive long after their menopause have more descendants. It's ruthlessly logical.

In non-human primates, females with declining repro-ductive abilities are often neglected by the group and die soon after menopause. Their living conditions deteriorate because they can no longer play an active role in the group. Jean-Jacques Hublin adds, 'If post-menopausal females have much higher life expectancies in humans than in monkeys, it's because for us humans they are a real benefit for the group. In the animal kingdom, nothing comes for free.' Humans probably protected older women in return for all the services rendered by these elderly women, a movement that archaeologists sometimes describe as 'empathetic'.

Indeed, *sapiens* were able to take advantage of these women for the benefit of all by assigning them a large share of responsibility in finding food. They even provided more calories than men, if we believe the statistics found among the Hadza people, where older women provide 30% of nutritional resources while older men provide only 5%. These women may bring in less protein, but they are reliable. As Kristen Hawkes says, let's not forget that 'in big game hunting, the chances of succeeding every day are extremely low. To be able to eat regularly, it's much safer to rely on gathering food and hunting small prey.'

So these older women are not a burden on their group, but an asset. What's more, 'the older women might have been a tremendous source of learning and knowledge. We are insatiable students and our big brains make us want to learn regularly and for a long time.' All the more reason for the group to devote energy to their survival.

Indeed, the transmission of complex knowledge needs time. From an evolutionary point of view, the survival of caring, wise women is privileged because the knowledge they transmit to the youngest members of the group helps to improve everyone's living conditions.

But when did all this start? When did the 'granny revolution' change the course of our evolution? While admitting that she can't draw up an exact timeline, Kristen Hawkes believes that this profound change 'began long before we become *sapiens*. We should be looking for it in the roots of the genus *Homo*, maybe 2 or 3 million years ago.'

This anthropological research sheds new light on what made us who we are. Fundamental to our humanity, the traits of empathy, sharing and collaboration have enabled the development of our species, our intelligence, our culture and our relationships. This is how *sapiens* succeeded on our planet at the expense of other species, acquiring its own special place.

For thousands of years, Lady Sapiens and her peers were influential mothers and grandmothers. And like prehistoric career women, they also made their mark on the world of work in these Paleolithic societies, just like the supposedly all-powerful male hunter.

Chapter 6

WOMEN ON ALL FRONTS

It's hard for people today to envisage the routine tasks our ancestors had to perform. Moreover, in traditional societies, the notion of 'work' is radically different from ours. It's difficult for us Westerners to imagine a system of production in which time cannot be monetized and working hours are not strictly scheduled. Paleolithic humans were undoubtedly far removed from these concerns, but the working hours of today's hunter-gatherers, as calculated by anthropologists, provide a few clues. Indeed, the Kung people of the Kalahari Desert in Namibia spend just 12 to 19 hours a week looking for food. This leaves them plenty of time to create craft items that are as useful as they are stylish, to express themselves through art, to share mythological tales by the fireside and to interact with loved ones without watching the clock. This way of life was probably embraced by humans in prehistoric times, leaving them free to create the incredible wealth of culture they have passed down to us.

In the hunter-gatherer groups of the Upper Paleolithic, cohesion and solidarity must have been essential for these small human communities to survive. And everyone, man or woman, had to contribute to a cooperative dynamic that ensured the smooth running of everyday life.

In the collective imagination, hunting remains the pre-eminent activity in prehistoric times, with men being regarded as the supreme suppliers of fresh meat. The theory of 'man the hunter', as presented at the eponymous 1966 conference by American scientists Richard B. Lee and Irven DeVore, reinforced this widespread image. Our investigations into the activities and habits of prehistoric women have revealed a completely different picture of our ancestors' daily occupations. They undertook a range of activities of unexpected variety, central to which hunting certainly occupies an important place, but isn't as dominant as we have been led to believe. Finding food was a job for both sexes, although women, as we will see, played a major role. As for the remainder of the time after a successful hunting or gathering expedition, it was most often devoted to basic household chores and to crafts in which, again, women certainly made an impact.

And we should not imagine that motherhood was an obstacle that prevented young mothers from participating in the life of the tribe, although a degree of ingenuity was needed to free up their hands. This early form of emancipation can be found in a revolutionary Upper Paleolithic device – the baby carrier.

Free Hands, Free Women

Carrying her baby on her back frees the mother's hands, allowing her to engage once again in group activities as soon as she has recovered from childbirth. Francesco d'Errico describes how these first baby carriers in human history were depicted on a stone plaquette found at the Paleolithic site of Gönnersdorf in Germany:

In their huts, Magdalenian hunter-gatherers used shale plaquettes to create a paved floor. On two of these plaquettes they carved animals and on others depictions of women. The number of women they drew here is impressive. There are four hundred images of females on some one hundred and twenty plaquettes found on the floor.

Such a profusion of works of art underfoot seems astonishing, but the prehistorian Romain Pigeaud offers an explanation:

These decorated plaquettes seem to have been reusable and recyclable. It's possible that they were engraved during ceremonies... then they were discarded when they were no longer needed, and used as hearthstones or paving stones... Then they were taken up again later to create a new engraving.

Left: Reconstruction of a baby-carrier inspired by ethnographic evidence from Native Americans. Right: One of the plaquettes found at Gönnersdorf, Germany shows a woman (central figure) with a baby carrier on her back (top left).

Looking more closely at these plaquettes discovered by Gerhard Bosinski, Francesco d'Errico draws our attention to an engraving of a baby carrier:

There is one plaquette on which we can clearly see a woman wearing a baby carrier on her back. This apparatus resembles those used by some Native Americans. It's a rigid structure that's separated from the wearer's back. It is possible that the baby carriers were decorated, because we can see some lines etched on this one.

These baby bags were a very practical invention for female Paleolithic hunter-foragers. Romain Pigeaud finds the existence of this type of artefact unsurprising: 'In traditional societies, women are not totally focused on their children – they know how to deal with them. The image of the woman at home trapped in her role as a mother is much more recent and seems hardly appropriate in prehistory.'

And ethnologist Michèle Coquet adds: 'Was prehistoric woman active? Of course. In any case, she didn't have a lot of other options.' Indeed, for a key member of the group such as Lady Sapiens, remaining aloof from the activities of the camp was surely impossible. Prehistoric woman assumed many roles, making her a career woman before her time.

Like the Hadza grandmothers studied by Kristen Hawkes in Tanzania's Lake Eyasi basin, prehistoric women would therefore have been crucially important for the group. But what exactly was their work? When we try to find out how the different daily tasks were distributed within prehistoric human groups, we very quickly come up against a very controversial concept – the sexual division of labour.

In Search of Women's Work

This anthropological theory is as old as the discipline itself. In their studies of certain non-Western populations – but still influenced by the model of European society in the late nineteenth century – ethnologists and subsequently prehistorians put forward the notion that women and men did not engage in the same activities. Some even argued that psychomotor and cerebral capacities were naturally allocated according to sex, and that over the centuries human societies invented norms to systematize access to a particularly activity for one or the other gender. This assertion gained traction over four decades of research into the sociology of work. But prehistory still presents uncharted waters when it comes to determining who was doing what in Lady Sapiens's encampment. Were prehistoric women restricted to certain activities?

The answer is far from clear. It's a complex issue trying to determine what women were doing using archaeological analyses, because a tool or an arrowhead is hardly going to be able to tell a scientist the gender of its creator and its user.

As a result, ethnographic comparisons have often been employed to answer this question, albeit using a dubious methodology. Instead of exploring all the populations that have been studied and providing exact statistics, early prehistorians allowed themselves to be swayed by a small number of particularly striking populations. For example, they cited the Inuit in particular in their hypotheses concerning the lifestyles of prehistoric groups, because they consume a lot of meat and because of the strict sexual division of labour that characterizes their society. They were quickly compared with our ancestors, who were considered to be big meat eaters who kept women in the home. Some scientists are still strongly attached to this theory and insist that it is just 'common sense' that women were not endangered by being allowed to take part in hunting, the outcome of which was often uncertain or even fatal. Yet we know today that, even among the Inuit, the roles of men and women were not so clear-cut, and could even be reversed. When a family had no boys, one of the girls took on the role of a boy, and vice versa.

Marian Vanhaeren of the PACEA laboratory in Bordeaux points out that there is nevertheless 'a biological difference between men and women. And we find these biological traits in the social roles attributed to each person.' The different physical capacities of men and women would make their respective actions more efficient according to the tasks they were allocated.

But not all scientists subscribe to this idea of a sexual division of labour, for example Marylène Patou-Mathis: 'I tend to prefer a distribution of tasks based on aptitudes and skills. And tastes too, why not! So I imagine more of a rational management of task distribution for maximum efficiency, but also to maintain a better collective atmosphere.'

Methods of investigating archaeological objects are becoming more and more precise, and as science progresses the management of daily tasks becomes clearer. This allows us to refine our understanding of the activities of prehistoric women and visualize as accurately as possible what their daily life was like. This is one of the big surprises that emerged from our investigation.

The body has a memory, and studying skeletal remains enables us to reconstruct the physical activities of prehistoric humans. Today, those scientists who know how to decipher a simple mark on a tooth or a toe are able to reveal Lady Sapiens's daily life powerfully and precisely. A particularly thorough investigation into the wear and tear of bones in female skeletons found at an archaeological site in the Middle East has even made it possible to reconstruct their working posture.

Among the daily activities that have aroused the interest of scientists, let's look first at the most iconic prehistoric activity – hunting.

Was Lady Sapiens a Hunter or a Forager?

As we have already seen, women were traditionally excluded from hunting in the models developed by early prehistorians, who considered this activity too dangerous and required a physical strength that they considered incompatible with femininity. In so doing they excluded women from the process of hominization, in which hunting seemed at that time to be the cornerstone.

However, our investigations reveal that prehistoric women had strong muscles, and that they were much stronger than most of the female *sapiens* who inhabit our planet today. Their activities had an impact on their skeletons as much as they did on men. Nevertheless, Sébastien Villotte argues that, in the sample of individuals he studied, these activity markers were not identical, revealing that the two sexes did not use their muscles in the same way: 'We can see a much greater asymmetry in men, usually on the right-hand side. This is a good indicator of a gendered division of activities. From this we can deduce certain one-handed activities carried out most likely by men.'

These one-handed activities, performed with only one arm, the left or the right, resulted in particular pathologies. For scientists, some of them are characteristic of throwing. But exerting a lot of stress on a single arm can be an element in lots of activities, such as hammering flint, using axes or adzes and, of course, wielding hunting weapons.

Jona Aigouy, 2020 French javelin champion in the 'Espoirs' category, describes the similarities between her sport and the use of the spear thrower, a revolutionary tool in the Upper Paleolithic:

I tried out the spear thrower, and there are strong similarities with javelin throwing. This is why we find the same pathologies in prehistoric fossils and in today's javelin throwers!

Throwing weapons is an activity that requires great skill as well as muscle and tendon resistance that is tested greatly by throwing techniques. Out on the track at her training ground at CREPS* in Saint-Raphaël, Jona Aigouy, who is very aware of the physical challenges of her sport and the traumas that have scarred her body, explains the principle:

We make use of the myotatic reflex. This involves stretching the muscle as far as possible to create an involuntary contraction. Because of this the javelin throw is a discipline that causes physical trauma. We often get shoulder and elbow injuries, such as tendonitis and pathologies affecting the nerves.

Young woman throwing an assegai with the aid of a spear thrower.

---

* In France, CREPS (Centre de ressources, d'expertise et de performance sportives) is a national training network for first-class athletes.

Fortunately for archaeologists, these soft-tissue pathologies also alter the bones to which the tissue is connected.
Sébastien Villotte can identify small tears in the bone
that appear as a result of injuries to the elbow joints of
our Paleolithic ancestors. In the sample he studied, the
injured bones turn out to be male in 95% of cases – it's an
interesting finding, but does not mean that only men were
hunters. And Sébastien Villotte adds, using his expertise
as a statistician: 'Ultimately we have very few skeletons
from this period. And what was true for Western Europe
at the end of the Upper Paleolithic was perhaps not the
norm elsewhere.'

The majority of archaeologists and anthropologists now
agree with this position, as Michèle Coquet says: 'Elsewhere
in the world, tasks are fairly evenly distributed. The category
distinction between "male hunter" and "female forager" is
not as clear-cut as that. Women may well have been called
upon to kill big game.'

In South America, recent discoveries that enjoyed exceptional media coverage seem to prove him right. The archaeological site of Wilamaya Patjxa, located at an altitude of
3,925 metres in the Puno district of Peru, was occupied by
humans around 8,000 years ago, a period when the Andean
peoples still made a living as hunter-gatherers. Five burial
sites were excavated, and six individuals exhumed. Two of
them were found with hunting tools: a man in his thirties
and a young woman under the age of twenty. The individuals'
sex was identified by analysing their amelogenin, a protein
found in tooth enamel that under close examination can
reveal the presence of the Y-chromosome.

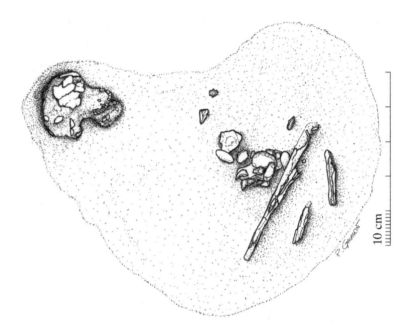

10 cm

The burial site of the young woman found at Wilamaya Patjxa,
Peru.

Twenty-four stone artefacts had been placed in the young
woman's tomb, comprising a toolkit of everything needed
to hunt and butcher big game: six projectile points, four
scrapers, a possible backed knife and several chipped flakes
of stone used for a variety of purposes. All the tools were
enclosed in a satchel which has not survived, but which we
know was decorated because of the traces of ochre present.

Was this woman really a hunter? For the South American
archaeologists there is no doubt, and they point out that
this burial of hunting weapons alongside women is not an
isolated phenomenon. Ten American sites from the Late
Pleistocene or Early Holocene (between 12,000 and 8,000
BCE) have yielded eleven burial sites where women have been

interred alongside weapons. While this number is relatively small, it nevertheless suggests that the model of relatively undifferentiated work may have existed among some of the early Americans.

Prehistoric woman was therefore quite capable of hunting. But did she have the right to do so everywhere in the world? When it comes to Paleolithic hunting, a paradigm has blocked the thinking of scientists for decades – the so-called 'blood taboo' theory.

This meant that within certain human groups, women are not allowed to shed blood when hunting. Women were associated with life, as they give birth and so must maintain a symbolic distance from the kill. Equally, women bleed during menstruation, which is said to heighten the repugnance felt by humans towards the idea of associating women with blood-thirsty hunting. Marylène Patou-Mathis describes this highly symbolic power:

> *Alain Testart put forward the hypothesis that there was a universal taboo that said it was dangerous to mix the blood of hunting animals with women's menstrual blood. It has also been said that the smell of menstrual blood can scare game away.*

Can we extend these observations concerning certain populations to prehistoric human groups? Should we believe that women have generally been excluded from hunting parties? Sébastien Villotte thinks that this hypothesis is plausible to a certain extent, since 'the use of perforating hunting weapons is the most gendered activity in human groups studied by ethnographers. […] This activity is more often practiced by men.'

Of course, as Sophie A. de Beaune reminds us, 'When it comes to prohibitions and taboos, what is applicable in one location is not necessarily applicable everywhere and at all times. In the case of the taboo against spilling animal blood, we can cite the counter-example of the Agta women of the Philippines, who hunt using bows and machetes.' So statistical findings alone cannot validate the hypothesis of a universal prohibition.

A taboo may have banned women from hunting among certain prehistoric groups, but it's highly unlikely that this taboo was absolute, in light of archaeological findings and ethnological observations. And even though women would not have been allowed to kill animals by shedding blood, it's unlikely that they were excluded from procuring animal protein.

Michèle Julien and her colleague Claudine Karlin have worked for many years on an exceptionally well-preserved site on the left bank of the Seine, a settlement whose excavations were begun by André Leroi-Gourhan. Michèle Julien describes the site:

The Pincevent site lies a few kilometres downstream from the present-day town of Montereau. For many generations it was occupied by groups of Magdalenian hunters, some 13,000 years ago. It is perfectly preserved thanks to very regular sediment deposits brought in by the high tides of the River Seine. [...] Hunters returned to this site for generations because it was located beside the river, in a very special place where there was a ford that enabled animals to cross the river from one bank to the other... The herds of reindeer used this route in their migrations.

Claudine Karlin explains how this natural route that helped the movement of reindeer turned into a death trap for these graceful animals:

Reindeer are easier to hunt when they are in water. They are good swimmers, but much weaker and slower in water than on land. The reindeer is also a gregarious animal, crossing lakes and rivers in groups... In addition, at this location, the valley becomes narrower, so large numbers of reindeer have to make the crossing in a restricted space... So it's an excellent spot for hunting reindeer.

All the activity of the encampment seems to be geared towards the same goal of hunting as many animals as possible in the least amount of time. Michèle Julien describes this camp, which was the subject of extensive excavations:

We found an entire camp covering 5,000 square metres. It comprised four habitation units, probably tents that were surrounded by peripheral workshops. We can show that there were links between the habitations and the peripheral buildings, that is that people worked not only in their dwellings, but also in the workshops outside. [...] A very large quantity of reindeer bones were found in these habitations... corresponding to approximately 76 reindeer, whose carcasses were brought into the camp in early autumn. [...] How many people would have had to live in this camp to make such a feat possible? And how long did they stay? This group consisted of around 30 people. They must have stayed there after the three or four weeks of hunting in order to deal with all the animals, because they had to take care of the carcasses.

One question remains unanswered: what contribution did women make to these large hunting parties? According to Claudine Karlin, 'we might imagine that the men were throwing spears at the game and that the women and children were driving the herd back towards the hunters' positions'.

Both the meat and the secondary products had to be processed quickly on site. All the members of the group had plenty to do, as Michèle Julien explains:

It's fine to kill all these reindeer, but then you have to cut them up, possibly cure the meat by drying it to have supplies for the winter. And then these animals had skins that had to be worked. The male reindeer have antlers, an extremely valuable raw material, especially for making spearheads and other tools... All of these activities were carried out immediately after slaughtering the animals in the camp.

Claudine Karlin goes further:

Seventy-six reindeer slaughtered in just a few weeks, that represents more than three tonnes of meat... This meat is cut up into quarters, probably on the riverbanks, then brought back inside the camp... and now the meat had to be processed, the antlers harvested, the hides prepared, and this suggests that the whole group had plenty to do during these few weeks. It seems to us that the position of women in this place of slaughter is essential.

Michèle Julien emphasizes that hide-working in particular 'takes days and days of work, because they have to be cleaned, dried, then washed again – it takes an extremely long time. And it requires a great deal of expertise.'

For the two scientists, it's easy to imagine that the women were part of these workshops while the men killed the reindeer. Western scientists rarely associate women with hunting, because this word still occupies a whole area of our medieval imagination. Hunting is seen as an athletic, dangerous activity – the fiercely physical, hazardous slaughter of giant beasts with sharp teeth and claws – or as training for war. It is of course difficult to imagine pregnant or breastfeeding women risking their lives in this kind of activity – it would hardly be a rational decision for the survival of the group.

But let's not forget that there are a number of strategies for obtaining meat: using a hide, pursuing or stalking until the decisive confrontation with the hunted animal. Trapping and collective hunting can also be practised by those whose lives must not be endangered. Claudine Karlin reminds us that 'Hare can be caught in snares, and young fawns by hand'.

In these different scenarios, it seems that women – as well as children – could take part in the collective effort of catching game (as long as the group was able to organize hunting drives or build traps). The dichotomy between 'man as hunter' and 'woman as gatherer' as described until the 1970s therefore seems like a caricature. There is no reason why prehistoric groups would have ignored the valuable help of half the adult population during the hunt. And even if they didn't always kill the animal, women may have helped find animal protein in other ways – setting traps, carrying carcasses, butchering game, etc. Michèle Coquet comments indignantly, 'The nineteenth-century imagination set up the mammoth hunt as a symbol of prehistoric hunting, but it's a misconception. Most of the food came as a result of women's activities: small-game hunting, gathering and foraging.'

According to Sophie A. de Beaune, small-game hunting seems particularly important because of its guaranteed yield. It is 'more reliable than big-game hunting, whose success is more uncertain'.

De Beaune also emphasizes that fishing, gathering shellfish or hunting small marine animals can provide a significant calorie intake which we too often overlook:

When we talk about food in prehistory, we focus too much on land animals... But the rivers and seas were also harvested. Although archaeology has long neglected the phenomenon, both sea and river fishing were widely practiced.

Indeed, if the produce of seas, lakes or rivers was underestimated by early prehistorians, it is in large part because their excavation methods were still unsophisticated. Fish vertebrae went unnoticed during the early explorations of prehistoric sites. Subsequently, improvements in excavation techniques made it possible to highlight the importance of many species of fish in our ancestors's daily life: the presence of their vertebrae leaves little doubt that they were eaten. Some artistic representations of these animals also show that they have been observed in great detail: such is the case of the Magdalenian salmon depicted in the Gourdan Cave or Elephant Cave in France, which appears to be covered in the lines of netting that were used to catch it.

Today scientists conclude that our ancestors were eating seafood 300,000 years ago. Consumption of shellfish and other aquatic produce contributed to the success of the flexible and opportunistic subsistence strategies adopted by hunter-gatherers who lived in coastal regions, especially since these foods are extremely healthy. They are rich in protein, vitamin D, fatty acids and iodine, which are essential for *Homo sapiens'* good health and very difficult to find in a land-based diet.

Our ancestors' menus would have included sea fish, river, lake and stream fish, as well as lots of shellfish and crustaceans. Franchthi Cave in Greece was the site of a seafood platter featuring limpets, mussels, cockles and two different types of oysters – flat and hollow. From winkles to whales – which were eaten by the inhabitants of the Nerja Caves in Spain 14,000 years ago – prehistoric people do not seem to have overlooked any of the marine animals they could lay their hands on without offshore navigation. When they couldn't fish for certain species that lived in the deep oceans, such as the whale, they would collect them from the shores where they sometimes beached. There is little doubt that women made a significant contribution to these activities, in particular foraging for bivalves, which was suitable work when looking after children, who must have enjoyed gathering them too.

In addition to their contribution to hunting, which is now difficult to deny, women also seem to have been queens of the plant world, and engaged in gathering. And indeed when we analyse the statistical data, this activity appears to be as rewarding as it is valued.

To ensure the group's livelihood on a regular basis, gathering was essential. 'We know from studying today's hunter-gatherer populations that these groups were largely dependent on small-game hunting and plant-based food, and these foods were collected by women.' These are the findings of James M. Adovasio, an archaeologist at the State University of Pennsylvania and a specialist in perishable artefacts.

Michèle Coquet confirms this observation, as the calorie density in the foods gathered by the San people of the Kalahari demonstrates: 'Women's contribution to the survival of the group is considerable. Among the San people, it has been shown that 75% of food intake is provided by women, while big-game hunting remains an exceptional event.'

Dani Nadel, professor of archaeology at the University of Haifa in Israel, also emphasizes the important role that women played in the survival of groups all over the world:

Since the 1960s, thanks to ethnographic and ethnoarchaeological studies, we know that women's contribution to the economy of tribes and families was much greater than previously estimated. This was because women were harvesting plant-based foods: cereal seeds, legumes, acorns and fruits depending on their environment. Their contribution to calorie and protein intake was sometimes between 50% and 70% of the group's average consumption at the time.

In the Middle East, women were also experts in wild cereals that they harvested to make flour by milling grains long before the invention of agriculture 10,000 years ago. And some resourceful archaeologists have managed to determine for certain that this work was carried out by women.

Humankind's First Women Millers

Welcome to Ohalo! This is where humans harvested a lot of wild cereals such as barley, wheat, oats, etc.

The discovery was made in Israel, at an exceptional 19,000-year-old archaeological site on the shores of Lake Tiberias. Led by Dani Nadel, the excavations uncovered six huts separated by circulation spaces. As Nadel explains: 'This site has been extremely well preserved because it has been underwater for a very long time. This meant we could make some incredible discoveries. Usually, we don't find seeds in sites from this period, but here we found hundreds of thousands.'

The discipline devoted to the study of ancient seeds is called carpology. It is one of the branches of archaeology that makes it possible to reconstitute plant environments of the past by identifying macro-remains of plants such as shell fragments, seeds or pips. But all this demands great care when collecting the evidence. All the archaeological sediment has to be sieved using water, then the seeds and plant particles are collected using the flotation technique, which consists of mixing the sediment with water and collecting the elements that float to the top.

Everything we could unearth was water-sieved using sieves with holes one-millimetre in diameter.

Using this method, the archaeologists realized that both the quantity and the diversity of the plant species our ancestors had collected on the site were impressive:

We were able to unearth more than one hundred thousand charred seeds from more than one hundred different species. We found trees such as tamarisk, oak, terebinth and dozens of species of edible grains and legumes. They were undoubtedly used for food.

The various occupations of the Ohalo II site were not seasonal encampments as is generally the case in prehistoric times. At Ohalo II scientists found the first signs of a sedentary lifestyle that would become the norm in the Middle East a few millennia later:

The plant remains found at Ohalo reflect every season of the year. We can also see this in the bird species: there are migratory birds, winter birds, etc. We know that humans lived in this camp for more than one season, maybe they even settled there for six months, a year, even two years... The encampment offers us different perspectives from what we are used to seeing in this period. If we think that staying for a year or two in one place is a sedentary lifestyle, then that's what was going on here.

Nevertheless, the occupants built nothing permanent. Their dwellings were modest huts made of perishable materials, surrounded by paths where a few fires had been lit. These somewhat small habitations were where women, the plant experts, may have indulged in some 'interior design':

In Ohalo, on the hut floor, our ancestors placed a very simple straw mat made of cereal plants. We also have evidence that some plants were brought to the site when they were in flower... Was this intentional? Were they used as decoration?

It was a common finding that people had made the most of these cramped living spaces:

The huts on the Ohalo site were not very spacious, but they were well organized. On one area of the floor, we could see shards of stone: we might imagine that one or two men sat there knapping flint. And in another area we found indisputable traces of food preparation...

By analysing how the remains were distributed within this space, the scientists could identify some very special tools:

On the floor we found a stone that at first seemed ordinary, in its natural state. It didn't attract our attention any more than that, but when we started to examine it, we discovered that it had been shaped, then fixed to the floor using sand and small pebbles so that it couldn't move. We also discovered an atypical pattern of cereal grains arranged around this stone: the seeds were placed around the stone at three points of the compass, as if someone had been crouching in front of the stone at the fourth compass point, and had been working the grains on the stone...

This is where the hypothesis of a grinding stone enters the discussion. But to verify that it was indeed a tool for grinding, the research team analysed the stone under the microscope: 'There were signs of wear and microscopic traces of starch and grain on it. So they probably used this stone to crush grains, make flour and prepare dough. This is without doubt one of the oldest examples of such activity.'

Bread became the staple food of human populations from the Neolithic period onwards, but it is exceptional to find evidence as old as this. Another notable discovery was made at Shubayqa in Jordan – a loaf of bread 'which dates back to about 14,000 years ago [...] made from cereal plants'.

All these unexpected findings don't tell us who might have been grinding this grain and baking this bread. However, Professor Nadel offers a hypothesis:

If we are to believe ethnographic studies, it is women who often know most about plants. ... They are often the ones who collect the seeds, the acorns, the fruits – all the natural foods that the family then eats. Was that the scenario here? We're not sure... but I believe so.

For Professor Nadel, there is a clear division of labour at Ohalo in which he imagines women to be naturally linked with the plant world and, by extension, with grinding, while men are engaged in stone-working. But imagination is not enough: for scientists, solid evidence has to be gathered. And a second site provides a more precise answer to these still unanswered questions.

We're now in Syria, at the site of Abu Hureyra. As at Ohalo, prehistoric people were gathering abundant quantities of wild cereals. This 9,500-year-old encampment has yielded up habitations and the particularly valuable remains of a necropolis. Some well-preserved bones have made it possible not only to identify the women in the group, but also to determine their working habits. Sophie A. de Beaune explains the evidence that was found:

In the necropolis, we found joint lesions on the ankles, knees, lower back and the base of the toes of a female skeleton. Now, these lesions correspond to dynamic and prolonged kneeling positions, and today they are commonly found among carpet-fitters.

Kneeling in order to grind cereals on a grinding stone fixed to the ground is a familiar feature of ethnographic and historical accounts. These fixed grinding stones might be quite similar to the so-called Ohalo grinding stone that was found still in its place inside a hut. Sophie A. de Beaune is convinced by the evidence:

We assumed that these women had to kneel to grind the grain on grinding stones on the ground, performing a back-and-forth movement. Well, several long grinding slabs for use with a back-and-forth movement were also found at the Abu Hureyra site, so we now have biological proof that it was indeed women who were grinding the grain.

*The skeleton of a young woman found at Abu Hureyra in Syria
presented joint lesions characteristic of grinding activity.*

If the women's work was the intensive processing of wild
cereals, it's a safe bet that they were perfectly well acquainted
with the reproductive cycle of seeds and ways of protecting
them. Now, many archaeologists believe that these plants
played a major role in early agriculture. Indeed, the cultivation
of cereals was invented in the Levant where the wild cereals
that were already widely used for food were growing. Can we
then argue that women launched the agricultural revolution?
Sophie A. de Beaune urges caution:

*It would be wrong to say that women 'invented' agri-
culture, because this process was very long. On the
other hand, women were very familiar with wild plants*

and how to use them. It is therefore likely that they contributed in a significant way to the emergence of agriculture.

Reconstruction of a sickle from the pivotal period between the Paleolithic and the Neolithic.

Professor Dani Nadel stresses that this question has long been a major concern of archaeologists:

Several scientists maintain that it was women first of all who had the brilliant idea of throwing or sowing seeds in order to grow food close to their dwellings. I think Darwin was among the first to write about this hypothesis some 150 years ago... This proves that it's a possibility that lingered in people's minds. But of course, it's impossible to say who had the idea first, man or woman... It's difficult to know for certain what happened 20,000, 12,000 or 10,000 years ago... But perhaps we have denied women a very important role in human evolution and in their contribution to the economy.

It's just a few steps from the fields to the grinding stone and from the grinding stone to the stove, steps that scientists did not hesitate to take. Were they right or wrong?

The Female Cook Feeds... Our Evolution

Linking prehistoric women with the daily preparation of food seems obvious to many ethnologists, since this domestic task is often performed by women in non-industrial societies, without being exclusively their domain. But we should beware of overly generalizing analogies that are in danger of fuelling clichés. Equally, an ethnographic model – even when dominant – should not suggest that men were systematically denied nurturing roles, just as today's hunter-gatherers should in no way be considered the direct descendants of prehistoric populations, as was thought in the nineteenth century. Nevertheless, it is very useful to draw on these models of populations living in symbiosis with nature and to remind Westerners that cooking, even when this activity takes place only within the domestic sphere, is in no way demeaning. We must never forget that the tasks that seem simple and ordinary to us today were fundamental to our ancestors. It was no more or less than a question of survival. In this sense, preparing meals for the group was of the utmost importance, and just as noble as bringing back game from the hunt. We should therefore reject the reductive image of the 'housewife' that was promoted by 1960s advertisements; we feel it's important to emphasize that the role of the prehistoric female cook was so essential that she made us *sapiens* what we are today.

Indeed, diet played a key role in the cognitive evolution of early humans and their ancestors. It was the consumption of meat and, much later, cooked meat that enabled the ancestors of modern humans to increase their brain size. This cause-and-effect relationship may seem surprising, but it's completely logical: the brain of modern humans consumes more than 20% of the energy expended by the whole body. Now, a diet that was sufficiently rich in calories and nutrients made it possible to satisfy the energy expenditure of the brain. Bigger brains gave rise to more complex social behaviour, which led to new foraging tactics and improvements in diet, which in turn promoted brain development, in what is called a process of coevolution. Later, cooking with fire improved the absorption of food and nutrients, relieving the pressure on the digestive system and making it less energy-hungry. If women were the group's feeders from the beginning, we should credit them with the cognitive advances that have revolutionized the development of humanity.

After thousands of years of evolution, our brains have become capable of producing social discourses and symbolic images. And it was over a meal prepared by female cooks that this discourse spread. Around fire and food, the bonds of the clan were strengthened, alliances forged and the myths of the ancients passed on. The meal is often a time of exchange whether familial, intellectual or emotional. It is the cement that binds a traditional human group, as Canadian scientist Brian Hayden points out in his recent book on prehistoric feasts, *Feasting in Southeast Asia* (University of Hawaii Press, 2016). With fingers literally in every pie, women were therefore the architects of communication between the members of the group, and essential to the flourishing of prehistoric civilizations.

One question remains, however. Was Lady Sapiens able to sharpen the knives she used to prepare the meals? This question, which archaeologists thought they had the answer to, has long been side-stepped, but today it is now being explored in more depth.

Women Stone-workers

The hypothesis that the prohibition preventing women from shedding blood stifled the idea that women might have been hunters; and similarly some powerful, ancient prejudices decreed that they could not be stone-workers. It is true that, in some traditional populations, women were banned from using piercing weapons and by extension from the manufacture of sharp weapons. This is why, in our school textbooks and museums, there are a multitude of illustrations and reconstructions, showing just men busily knapping flint. But what do we really know about this subject?

No scientific method exists that can distinguish a tool made by a woman from a tool made by a man. Lithic tools are not gendered. In the Paleolithic, there was no reason for women to be excluded from stone-working, at least not because of their lack of muscle power. Shaping flint or obsidian requires above all a long and rigorous apprenticeship, dexterity and intelligence, qualities shared by both men and women.

Yet statistics in ethnological studies show that women are allocated stone-working activities much less frequently than men. In a comparative study of several contemporary populations, stone-working was identified as a male activity in 67 societies and as a female activity in only 6 populations, notably 'among the Konso of Southern Ethiopia, the Arawe people of New Guinea and the Tiwi and Jerramungup of Northern and Western Australia', as Marylène Patou-Mathis explains.

What was the situation in Europe 30,000 years ago? Did Lady Sapiens work flint to make tools? To answer this question, Claudine Karlin carried out a comparative study:

We embarked on a project to live among the peoples of Siberia, observing diverse populations during different seasons. The climate was not the same, the altitude was not the same and neither were the populations... So we were able to recognize various attitudes and differentiate between what might be the result of environmental constraints and what might be personal choice... and therefore be part of the culture.

Based on observations of the Dolgan population, Karlin conjectures that in winter the men would go hunting, leaving the women alone in the camp for several days. It was therefore impossible that women were dependent on men when it came to making their everyday tools.

Michèle Julien believes that what she observed at the Pincevent site is compatible with her colleague's hypothesis:

There were a number of objects scattered around the hearth: flint tools, stones, a certain quantity of kitchen scraps... Life as a whole centred on this fire. But it seemed to us that there were two spaces on either side of the hearth... One side was for expert stone-workers, the other for a worker who was less dextrous but who was also working on bones and hides. We therefore surmised that the first space was for men and the other for women.

In the space the scientists assumed to be female, there were scrapers, pebbles used for polishing, lissoirs or smoothers, but also a small needle-making workshop:

In this 'female' space, we could see that the stone-worker was not highly skilled in knapping flint. The tools weren't 'great'... but they were good for carrying out lots of every-day tasks.

Another find supports the hypothesis that Pincevent had a space reserved for a multi-talented woman:

Just next door to the 'female' area, we found a small concentration of debitage which is made up of 'flakes' – small pieces of stone chipped off in a haphazard way. These flakes came from a pebble that had been deliberately shattered: it is highly typical of a child playing in imitation of adults. We got the sense that alongside this woman who was knapping flint was a little child who had also picked up a flint, and who was striking it in a random way to imitate his mother – who could work in this area and keep an eye on her child at the same time.

For some scientists, stone-working in the Paleolithic seems to be a predominantly male activity, with women doing it to meet immediate technical needs. But all scientists agree on one point: it seems inconceivable that women did not know how to knap stone, if only to maintain a certain independence in their day-to-day work. As lithic tools were used in all areas of life, denying women a part in their production would mean she was not allowed to cook, engage in hide-working, or create objects out of bone or wood. It is therefore obvious that Lady Sapiens must also have been a stone-worker in order to carry out her daily tasks. Was she, however, able to create the beautiful Solutrean laurel-leaf blades, those exceptionally finely worked hand axes? This becomes less likely when we consider all the other tasks she was already responsible for. But it is no longer inconceivable, as was the case until recently.

Essential Craft Skills

In this age of mass production and free-market economies, we find it hard to imagine how essential certain crafts are to the survival of an entire group. We have forgotten that a watertight shoe could save our toes when we're out walking in the snow, or that a sturdy, finely woven basket makes for efficient gathering. The techniques of artisanal production, often managed by women in traditional societies, are valuable assets in everyday life.

If we are to believe ethnographic studies, women seem to be in charge of the world of plants, as we have already seen. Now, plants enable the development of a considerable number of crafts. Their qualities are just as varied as raw materials of animal origin. Flexible, resistant and elastic, wood, reeds or simple leaves can be used for making both clothes and huts, vessels for cooking food and baskets for transporting goods or babies. Some other primates in the animal kingdom are very well aware of this, as chimpanzees use the specially prepared tips of twigs to dig out termites from deep within their mounds.

James Adovasio decided to look into the analysis of these little-understood remains:

Unlike stone or ceramics, which don't break down, organic materials are rarely found by archaeologists, because they are subject to bacterial decay, except in very specific conditions, in very wet soils for example... but generally they break down very quickly.

For Adovasio 'the development of technology using plant materials took place sporadically before our era... but it grew exponentially with the arrival of our species, *Homo sapiens*, and more particularly thanks to women'.

It's true that all these materials constitute a very important part of the technologies used by traditional populations. Professor Adovasio has observed this on many occasions: 'For the majority of today's hunter-gatherers, technology made from perishable materials constitutes more than 90% of the objects in use. These materials are turned into fabric, leather, basketry, wood and woven plant fibres.'

We must remember that these are not easy tasks: they require an in-depth knowledge of the material and an organization of labour based on a complex chain of production. James Adovasio emphasizes this aspect:

We know that objects made of perishable materials are produced over several stages… There is no reason why we should give more status to a flint blade than to wicker baskets… but as the latter leave fewer traces, we often overlook them.

Our perspective on everyday objects made by prehistoric populations is thus biased because organic materials conserve so poorly. Time has removed them from our sight – and from our minds. For James Adovasio this is a source of regret, and he has dedicated his career to changing our perceptions:

People think it was middle-aged men who were in charge of life in the camp and who killed the big beasts using flint tools. This has been our view of the prehistoric world since the nineteenth century… but it's not true! We have been stuck with this belief until now because the things women produced are invisible to archaeology… […] Using ethnographic comparisons, we know that the production of basketry, objects made from plant material as well as much of the production of wooden objects, was carried out by women in all pre-industrial societies. Of course, that does not mean that men were unable to perform these kinds of tasks…

Indeed, James Adovasio is certainly not out to denigrate men's work. For a very long time, men seem to have been in the majority in certain sectors of activity:

We have photographs taken during World War II that show Japanese soldiers making their own sandals. Moreover, shoe-making has always been a mainly male activity, although no one knows why. But as for the rest of the items made from perishable materials, women are the prime artisans.*

This opens up multiple perspectives. For example, we recall the imprints of plant fibres found on terra-cotta fragments in Dolní Věstonice. These exceptional traces were examined by James Adovasio. He explains the extraordinary process that made their conservation possible:

These remains have survived because they were pressed and imprinted on clay... which was then baked by being near a fire. The imprint of this craftsmanship has been preserved thanks to it being exposed to heat, otherwise it would have been lost. [...] In Central Europe, we find only imprints of woven items. This is one of those occasions when the archaeologist gets lucky. We don't find the object itself... but rather a negative imprint of the object on another object which has been preserved.

But what were these mysterious objects whose imprints have been preserved in the clay? It didn't take long for Professor Adovasio to realize that these were 'remains of plant material woven in a very similar way to the shirt you or I are wearing'.

---

* Among the Inuit, however, it is the women who make the boots. This is also a very important criterion for a man when he comes to choosing a partner. A woman who makes comfortable, waterproof boots is a great asset when it comes to seal hunting on the pack ice.

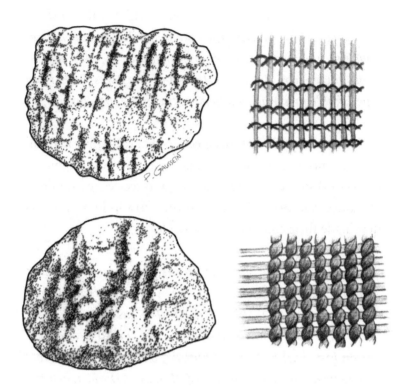

Textile imprints found at Dolní Věstonice and
their possible reconstruction.

As to how and why this textile was woven, we cannot be sure, because the imprints were very small. They are perhaps fragments of clothing or bags that prehistoric people found very useful when out gathering.

Even without knowing the nature of the final object this woven textile constituted, 'we can still identify the techniques that were probably used to create these objects', James Adovasio adds on a brighter note. 'The threads are wound around themselves like a rope, then they are woven on a vertical weft, probably stretched over a frame.'

Before the fibres can be woven, the raw material must be prepared. To do this, women knew how to use their nimble hands as well as their teeth.

Weaving is not the only activity whose traces have disappeared from excavation sites. Sophie A. de Beaune notes that 'in the Neolithic levels of the Syrian site of Abu Hureyra, we found a female mandible with grooves on the teeth. We might imagine that this woman must have used her teeth to prepare vegetable fibres, stripping rushes of their outer skin to use them in basketry.'

So in prehistoric times weaving and basketry were already activities that required perseverance and dexterity. But it was worth the effort, because the objects created were vital, as James Adovasio points out:

Objects made from plant fibres were essential to the survival of these groups. They were part of the totality of prehistoric social activities and were of considerable importance. Woven fibres can be used to transport food of plant origin, to make cooking and baking utensils, to create mats or animal traps, to make blankets or clothes for the summer period, when it was hot... The general public thinks that it was perpetually cold during prehistoric times, but it really was not. So there were times of the year when lighter clothes were needed, clothes that couldn't be made of fur. The image of men and women always wearing furs is a stereotype that has remained with us for far too long.

Over the course of our investigation, we have realized the extent to which prehistoric clothing was sophisticated and socially meaningful. If women had a particular connection with the plant material used to weave baskets and clothes, it is quite possible that it was also female hands who did the sewing. From Pierre Cardin to Alexander McQueen, our greatest fashion designers have often been men, but it's safe to say that women played an important role in creating the wardrobes of the past. Female work often became male when it gained in prestige and took place outside the domestic sphere. Pottery and weaving in Africa are good examples of this.

As Francesco d'Errico emphasizes, in the past, archaeologists had no difficulty describing the sexual division of labour in this context: 'Traditionally, it was thought that it was women who made the bone needles because this is what we observed among the Inuit or Amerindian populations...'

Nevertheless, can we derive an anthropological constant from this fact? Was sewing woman's work? Among the populations studied by ethnologists, certain activities seem most likely to be female, as is the case with textile crafts. However, some counter-examples make it impossible to imagine that this activity was strictly out of bounds for men. In sub-Saharan Africa, for example, weavers are generally men. Francesco d'Errico suggests we should remain open-minded about every possibility: 'It's likely that the needles were used by women, but it's possible that the men worked with them too... or even produced them.'

Let's not forget that today, Icelandic men know how to make knitwear with intricate floral patterns just as well as women. For these men, the gender division of this task is meaningless, and they are just honouring a centuries-old tradition. The same may have been the case for members of certain prehistoric groups for whom the art of beauty was not the preserve of Lady Sapiens alone.

Indeed it's true that the diversity of materials used by prehistoric couturiers for their impressive creations sometimes resulted in some very sophisticated clothes. To accompany this finery, prehistoric people also created a range of jewellery that was quite the equal of our own. We now know that jewellery was not just for women. But equally, was jewellery-making an activity undertaken by both sexes? It's quite possible, since, according to Michèle Coquet, 'there is no such clear division of tasks between the sexes, but rather a kind of permeability. Men too can sew, create personal ornaments, and use body paint.'

However, some prehistoric jewellery seems to have been made by people with very small hands. Of course, this characteristic is not exclusive to women, but Randall White believes that it was women who created the beads found in Le Cellier rock shelter in the Dordogne:

We found lots of very delicate beads: they are tiny, with an average circumference of 6 mm. We reconstructed the process in experiments, and it must have taken three hours of work on average to make each of these beads. [...] I have relatively normal hands for a man and I can't make the tiniest of these beads... I simply can't hold them firmly enough in my hand to work on them. By contrast, the vast majority of my female students can do the job. This seems to support the idea that this activity was predominantly female.

Weaver, seamstress, jeweller – few activities seem beyond the reach of prehistoric women, not to mention that hide-working is also associated with the female domain. Here again, evidence of deterioration in female mandibles has produced some interesting clues: the incisors may have been used as a sort of third hand in weaving, but also as a tool in hide-working. In some traditional societies, women habitually chew skins to soften them. For the Tigara people who lived in Point Hope, Alaska, between 750 and 250 BCE, their front teeth were essential tools for softening animal skins and making thread from tendons. It's a habit they may have inherited from prehistoric times, as scientists Katarzyna Górka, Alejandro Romero and Alejandro Pérez-Pérez have shown.* Likewise, another study, based on Almudena Estalrrich and Antonio Rosas's analysis of nineteen Neanderthal skeletons, was able to show that women used their front teeth much more than men for non-food activities. It's an early clue to thinking about the sexual division of labour in prehistory.

Pottery appeared in the Neolithic period around 7,500 BCE, but there were precedents to this invention. Indeed, the firing of clay has been recorded as early as the Upper Paleolithic at three Central European sites, two of which are dated to around 27,000 years old and a third, more recent, dated between 19,500 and 17,500 years old. These are, of course, independent inventions. We have already mentioned one of the most beautiful clay Venus figurines of Central Europe, that of Dolní Věstonice. Undoubtedly this technique did not

---

* 3. See Katarzyna Górka, Alejandro Romero and Alejandro Pérez-Pérez, 'Dental-Macrowear and Diet of Tigara Foragers from Point Hope, Northern Alaska' in *Anthropologischer Anzeiger* (2016), vol. 73, no. 3, pp. 257–64.

continue beyond the Paleolithic and did not lead to practical applications such as pottery later on. Some scientists suggest this significant shift was due to a female invention. What if the first potters were women? According to Dani Nadel, in certain locations there is no doubt:

At a few Pavlovian sites in the Czech Republic, small ceramic objects were made that were probably fired in an oven – in particular, some very delicate animal and human figurines… According to the fingerprints found on these objects, the last people to have handled them before firing were predominantly women. This would mean that women would have had a very specific role in the making of these small animal figurines mainly depicting mammoths.

Pottery in our usual understanding of the word was not invented until much later, by the first farmers of the Near Eastern Neolithic, and it is fair to say that it changed our ancestors' lifestyles. By enabling new ways of preserving food and cooking, pottery revolutionized everyday life. But when we look at this from an ethnological point of view, the gender division in pottery-making is much less evident than in stone-working or working with plant material. As with cooking and sewing, it seems that pottery became a male activity when it left the domestic sphere and professionalized.

If women did indeed practice all these arts, it's clear that they contributed greatly to the improvement in living conditions and the overall technological progress of humankind. Weaving plant material enabled the development of basketry. This in turn enabled the creation of all kinds of receptacles for fishing, gathering berries and other plant material on a large scale, and for transporting objects and even babies. Sewing hides together served to protect against the cold, to make covering for tents and vessels for conserving liquid or solid food. Later on, pottery made it possible to transport commodities in greater quantities and further afield. Through these crucial, productive activities women thus played an essential role not only in the survival but also in the cultural development of prehistoric groups.

Women Artists

Turning now to prehistoric art, very early on scientists were struck by some wonderful cave paintings and engravings. Yet for a long time, the identity of those who created these works was not even questioned, as if, in all likelihood, only men had a monopoly on the earliest artistic creations in our history.

The question is nevertheless a valid one: could women in the Upper Paleolithic have been artists? This hypothesis did not occur to the early prehistorians of the nineteenth century who lived in a world where women could still not aspire to equality when it came to making images. At the end of the century, women were still not allowed to take certain courses at Paris's École des Beaux-Arts, in particular, for reasons of decency, the life-drawing classes that featured nude male models. However, Michèle Coquet shows that in many populations women are regarded as real artists:

> There are women painters among the Congo Pygmies: they use sap to paint abstract patterns on flattened tree bark... Among the Aboriginal Australians, the female elders have

their own inventory of body painting and also draw patterns on the ground during ceremonies.

So can we not imagine prehistoric women being sculptors or painters? After all, they have always occupied a special place in prehistoric art as a favourite theme. From the delicate faces drawn on the plaquettes found in the Cave of La Marche to the sculpted Venus figurines of the Gravettian period, women have been a source of inspiration. And it's possible that some of them posed for artists. An American scientist has even hypothesized that Paleolithic women were depicting themselves by looking at their bodies from above, which would explain the distorted representation of certain body parts. Most prehistorians consider this idea to be absurd – surely women only needed to look at other women to know their own anatomy – but the role of women in art is now being seriously investigated.

Before imagining women as workshop masters like the Leonardos of ancient times, we might first look at their role in acquiring the materials to create works of art. Indeed, as we have seen earlier, Upper Paleolithic artists were willing to use rare and exotic pigments, and long expeditions were sometimes necessary to acquire them. Now, nothing was stopping women, who could walk long distances just as well as men, from joining these groups, but no evidence has been found that could confirm this either.

Whatever the case, the attention given to acquiring pigments and dyes clearly shows the degree to which aesthetic creativity occupied an important place in the symbolic and social systems of human groups of the period. The time spent making elaborate wall paintings, such as those depicting dappled horses in Pech Merle cave in the Lot, leaves little room for doubt. When we look at this famous panel, we can see negative handprints framing the animal figures. They were made using a stencil technique – the artists pressed their hands against the cave walls then blew pigment around them. So who did these 'negative' hands belong to? Advances in biology may well provide an answer.

Dean Snow, professor of anthropology at the University of Pennsylvania, set out to identify the sex of the negative handprint artists, using the digit ratio which says that the ratio of index finger length to ring finger length is not the same in men as in women. Using morphometric analysis software, Snow and his team took up the challenge of measuring prehistoric hands on cave walls. The task was fraught with pitfalls, because, as Sophie A. de Beaune rightly points out, 'most of the negative handprints are incomplete... and therefore difficult to analyse using the digit ratio'.

It was possible to analyse only thirty-two complete hands found in eight caves, including El Castillo in Spain, Gargas and Pech Merle in France. And it turned out that twenty-four of them were female. At Pech Merle, they are positioned just below the majestic horses with their famous dappled rumps.

So we can conclude that women took part in some way in the creation of some of the parietal art. But we would be mistaken in thinking that one day we will be able to quantify the number of female artists who worked in these caves.

What did the presence of these female hands near the art works mean? Were they signatures, like those Aboriginal painters who sign their works using their fingerprints? This hypothesis, which would allow us to say that these women were indeed the artists, has seemed attractive to many scientists. But there is nothing to say for certain that the creators wanted to assert their identity alongside their works, especially as some handprints appear on their own. It's possible that they may have had a purely decorative function or, as in other cases found around the world, that they were simply there to mark the artist's presence, like modern graffiti. In any case, the presence of female handprints shows that women frequented the caves, braving the darkness alongside men. And other kinds of prints have also been found which confirm this.

We followed the prehistorian Philippe Galant down the winding passages of the Cave of Aldène, in Hérault, to decipher the clues that indicate the presence of prehistoric humans. Along the way, he showed us torch marks on the cave wall – more precisely, burnt coal. For Galant, these were deliberate marks made to indicate the way – nothing less than a trail of breadcrumbs to help us find our way out of the cave easily after our exploration. They have allowed archaeologists to pinpoint the depth to which individuals ventured in these underground spaces. But this was not the only finding.

Careful analysis of these marks has revealed to scientists the morphology of our ancestors' torches. Between ten and sixteen small pieces of juniper wood were gathered into a bundle. This fact is not insignificant because, by reproducing these torches and lighting them, it has been possible to re-enact the length of time the equipment could illuminate the expedition of these prehistoric people. As Philippe Galant explains, 'A torch can emit light for between thirty and forty minutes. By adding up the marks made during their journey, we realized that they must have spent up to three or four hours underground. It was a real journey of exploration.'

And an adventure in which women played a role just as much as men. To find out, we just need to look down at the mud:

Here, stretching over a distance of 30 metres, we've found footprints. Between five hundred and six hundred footprints in all. We identified various different sizes and morphologies – children, adolescents and a few adults. Around twenty people, twenty-six, according to the trackers.

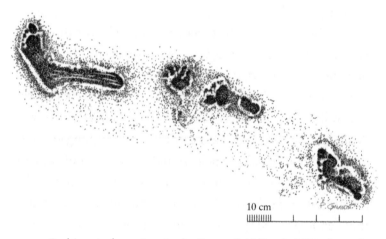

Prehistoric footprints in the Cave of Aldène in Hérault.

Philippe Galant, accompanied by Andreas Pastoors of Erlangen University in Germany, wanted to compare the results they had obtained through their clever calculations with data that had been obtained in a more traditional way. 'We brought in Namibian trackers who could offer a perspective that would complement our archaeological approach. Their approach is much more sensory than ours, and is based on life-long experience.' A research programme focussing on the footprints was thus set up to carefully record an inventory, characterize the individuals present, and describe the movements of the walkers.

The scientists had the trackers work blind – that is, without giving them any background information – in order to compare their impressions with their own test results.

It's quite a science! They have had to use tracking since their childhood because their lives depend on it. They have acquired all kinds of knowledge and can identify the physical movements associated with each footprint.

It took the trackers eight days of work to reconstruct the identity of the Paleolithic walkers. Their observation methods and their hypothesis validation protocols also impressed the scientists: 'Like us, they apply Cartesian analysis to empirical remains. They can be wrong, of course, but so can archaeologists.'

Women were indeed among the group. The trackers were even able to determine that one of them had free hands on the way in, but must have been carrying a heavy burden on the way back, because her feet sank deeper and her steps were less stable as a result of the extra load. What might she have been carrying? Rocks? Clay? What if she were simply carrying on her back a young child whose footprints were clearly visible on the way in but which were absent on the return trip? Tired after such a long walk, the toddler will probably have asked to be carried.

In the absence of tangible elements, only basic scientific caution is left: 'Often we've been thinking that cave artists were men,' Sophie A. de Beaune reminds us. 'We cannot say that women were the authors of the magnificent paintings at Lascaux, Pech Merle or Chauvet. But we cannot say that men were, either. There is no scientific evidence either way.'

If women were artists in any way, did their talent give them dominance over the other members of the group? Sophie A. de Beaune is not sure: 'Artists probably had a specific status. Can we go so far as to say that they had a particular "power" – that's somewhat hard to say.'

The practice of art was probably valued by prehistoric groups, because it's impossible to imagine that artists could have achieved this level of technical knowledge and experience without thousands of hours of training. Admiring the female sculptures of the Roc-aux-Sorciers rock shelter, Geneviève Pinçon emphasizes the advantages that prehistoric artists must have benefited from in order to fully devote themselves to their discipline.

If she's a sculptor, her time was organized to allow her to produce art, and she must have been an important person in her group. I think everyone's talent was spotted to serve the group in the interests of all.

The Many Talents of Lady Sapiens

After our long quest for prehistoric female activities, the role of Lady Sapiens emerges more clearly, despite the few uncertainties that persist. The parallels between ethnographic data and the archaeological remains themselves provide valuable models, but this is not always enough, because direct, compelling evidence that a task was performed by a man or a woman is extremely rare. And each situation that has been analysed can be exceptional as well as normal, so we must be careful not to engage in over-hasty generalizations.

In any case, there is no doubt that prehistoric women were extremely active and versatile, just like men. It is moreover very likely that, within such small groups, specialization was not commonplace, because it was hardly favourable to survival in emergencies. So, just as it seems absurd to imagine women being limited in their activities because they did not know how to produce a flint flake, it seems impossible to believe men were unable to prepare food when women were not around. The wholesale categorization of activities is often the prerogative of societies with a large demographic. Individuals may have been able to provide specialized work that fulfilled a particular desire or talent, but resourcefulness was surely an essential skill for all members of the community. Far from a relationship of dependence between individuals, it is more plausible to imagine a relationship of partnership, a kind of cooperation between everyone who shared out tasks according to skills. These were human communities where, as we have seen, men and women did not live exclusively from hunting – far from it.

And it is likely that the roles assigned to one or the other sex were not as distinct as early prehistorians wanted to believe. As we pointed out at the beginning of this chapter, modern Inuit were first studied through the distorting prism of an absolute sexual division, before a more rigorous approach made it possible to appreciate the flexible and common-sense organization of their society. Likewise, we can now abandon our prejudices in an attempt to tackle the question in terms of prehistory.

It is quite possible that the management of sexual identities was much more open and tolerant during prehistoric times than today. Lady Sapiens could perhaps help advance the dismantling of gender stereotypes that our own society is undergoing.

Chapter 7

POWERFUL WOMEN

Lady Sapiens was undoubtedly a woman of action. Thanks to knowledge-sharing between archaeology, anthropology and ethnography, we now know that she was involved in many daily activities essential to the survival of her group, as nurturer, huntress, forager, craftswoman, artist and perhaps more besides.

Recent discoveries have shed light on her privileged status among the tribes of the Upper Paleolithic, indeed prehistorians consider that Lady Sapiens could sometimes have been a powerful woman. But how can archaeologists find evidence of this? Power, like emotion, does not create fossils. Yet tremendous progress in the field of archaeology is opening up new areas of interpretation. The first challenge is to identify what forms of power existed in Lady Sapiens's era.

Power in Hunter-gatherer Societies

Women had a high status, that's for sure... but it's hard to know what it was.

What *it was* or what *they were*? Can we move beyond this question posed by Catherine Schwab and identify Lady Sapiens's social status?

Today scientists have the resources to answer this question to a certain extent. There is no reason why women did not take part in the group's important activities, so they were able to occupy 'positions of responsibility' in the same way as men.

We have to wait until the Neolithic era, around 10,000 BCE, and the Metal Ages in particular, before we see any kind of economic power emerging. At that time, certain individuals had privileged access to raw materials and to networks for distributing goods. In the Paleolithic, trade links already existed between remote groups, but these human units were small and so such exchanges did not have to be regulated by an authority figure. The wealthy merchants and mining bosses had yet to make an appearance. However, it is possible that certain individuals, whether men or women, may already have had specific responsibilities that reflected a certain degree of power, depending on their aptitudes or their inclinations for particular activities. Michèle Coquet points out that 'among hunter-gatherers, some women achieve a particular status depending on what they have been in life, for example when they have helped the group to survive in difficult situations'. This suggests the possibility that Lady Sapiens may have been particularly honoured among her group, being recognized for her many talents.

How did Paleolithic women acquire prestige and respect among their female peers? The lives of hunter-gatherers were probably as unpredictable as ours: twists of fate, whether good or bad, affected the group's existence on a daily basis. In the event of illness, people relied on the power of the healer and his or her mainly herbal remedies; when a conflict arose, it was invaluable to have a calm individual who used measured language, a mediator who was able to restore harmony. In times when food was in short supply, the skilful hunter would prove indispensable. Faced with trials that could not be overcome by any particular talent (natural or meteorological disaster, epidemics affecting game, etc.), there may have been individuals who could contact the spirit world or higher powers – individuals commonly known as shamans – although their existence is purely hypothetical. And ethnography tells us that female shamans are known to exist among certain populations.

Let's see what science tells us, more specifically, about the power of our ancestors.

Women in Charge?

Did our prehistoric ancestors create the first chiefdoms? Did dominant personalities who had a particular decision-making power within the group already exist in the Paleolithic? Michèle Coquet thinks that trying to find out who the leaders in prehistory were may be anachronistic:

Hunter-gatherer societies are relatively egalitarian. It's often inappropriate to talk about a 'leader', even if there are individuals who become essential because of their talents as hunters or their ability to resolve conflicts within the group. A woman could certainly have held such a position.

This status would have brought with it benefits, prestige and respect. For example, among populations living around the Arctic Circle, meat is allocated according to individuals' importance: the best cuts – the fattiest – go to the most respected, distinguished guests, elders, etc. According to Michèle Coquet, 'it is quite possible to imagine that women acquired a position of "advisor" in their community. Someone who is asked to make decisions for the group because she is capable, intelligent and unifying in the life of the community.'

In prehistoric societies that were sophisticated and responsive to imagery (see Chapter 3), important individuals had to be identifiable at first glance. It is therefore legitimate to think that men and women who took care over their personal ornaments did so to highlight their distinction within society. Moreover, exotic and therefore rare clothing or ornamentation are often a sign of special status. In the case of the Upper Paleolithic, it is in the most elaborate burials that a number of clues emerge; power in itself may not create fossils, but some signs of status can accompany the dead to their last abode. Dani Nadel explains that in their burials, women were no less well-endowed than men:

Near the kibbutz of Ein Gev, there's a 21,000-year-old site… where we found a hut in which a woman had been buried. She was curled up and there was a large basalt dish next to her, which might be a clue as to who she was. So women and men were buried with the same degree of respect – maybe because they had similar functions.

Other examples of Paleolithic burials make the case for the existence of individuals with privileged, even prestigious status, regardless of their gender.

The Magnificent Lady of Cavillon

The Lady of Cavillon was found in the Balzi Rossi Caves complex in Italy. The site harbours an initial, valuable clue that reveals the respect that the tribe had for this woman. Professor Henry de Lumley's sense of wonder has not diminished over time, as he describes how this burial probably took place:

This woman certainly occupied an important role in society. When she died at the age of thirty-seven, she was buried magnificently – not everyone was buried so royally. At the entrance to the Cavillon Cave, this lady was given a very elaborate funeral rite involving horses. An awl made of horse bone had been placed in front of her face; above the burial site, a pendant carved from a horse's metapode (foot bone) was found; 1.60 metres above the ground, a magnificent horse had been engraved on the cave wall.

In addition to this horse engraving, several remarkable objects accompanied the Lady of Cavillon in death: two thin blades carved from flint found in a quarry more than 150 kilometres from the cave and, in particular, a headdress woven with Mediterranean shells, and edged with a hundred canine teeth from male and female deer. Just before it was buried, the body was completely covered with red ochre.

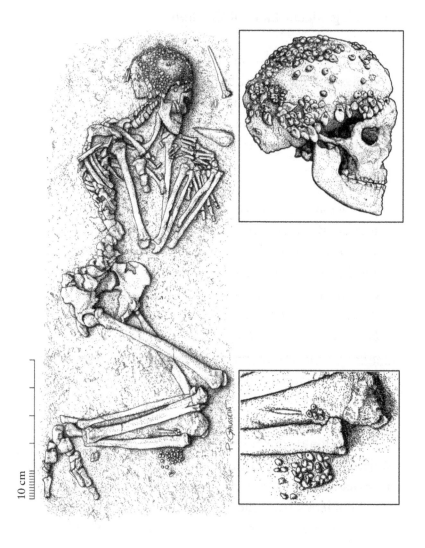

*Burial site of the Lady of Cavillon as discovered by Émile Rivière
in the eponymous cave in Liguria in 1872.*

A burial is the product of work undertaken by the group, and therefore testifies to the respect that its members give to the deceased. As Antonella Traverso, curator of the Balzi Rossi Museum, near the cave where the Lady of Cavillon was discovered, emphasizes:

Why did a prehistoric community, a community of the living, forgo objects such as flint blades or very beautiful, elaborate ornaments that were still useful to them, and give them to this woman? Why deny yourself these precious objects, for which you had to travel many kilometres and go to so much trouble? In my opinion, these people must have believed that they would be useful to the deceased during her passage into the world of the invisible. Indirectly this tells us that there was a kind of spirituality in these prehistoric communities, providing the most influential members, like the Lady of Cavillon, with essential items for their journey, for their life after death. The community of the living had a very great deal of respect for this woman.

Another burial, that of Saint-Germain-la-Rivière, provides powerful evidence of these privileged post-mortem processes that were granted to important people.

The Sleeping Beauty of Saint-Germain-la-Rivière

The Saint-Germain-la-Rivière site is a rock shelter in Gironde, located at the foot of a cliff in the Dordogne valley. About 15,700 years ago, during the Magdalenian period, a group of people came here to bury a woman.

This exceptional find revealed a proper tomb which had been dug to preserve the body of the deceased. The bones had not been disturbed although millennia had passed, a sign of the special care that had been taken to keep the body safe from attack by scavengers. Marian Vanhaeren describes the museum reconstruction of this last resting place, which 'belonged to a young adult, a woman. She was well protected, with two stone slabs around her and two slabs above her.'

The deceased 'was curled up in a foetal position', a common funerary position at that time. Around her, there was a quantity of precious goods: 'lots of ochre and body ornaments'.

Her clothes and her jewellery included more than seventy deer canines. The teeth had been carefully selected for their shape in order to form pairs. Scientists were able to determine that at least sixty-five different deer were the source of the canines used in this woman's ornamentation. And these teeth had not been not chosen at random: 'These animals were mostly young males, who produce the most beautiful canines.'

These objects had been accumulated over a long period of time as a result of various transactions. This hypothesis is not surprising if we consider that the burial site was created at a time when deer had abandoned the region as it had been totally deforested due to the prevailing cold conditions. The canines in the grave of the Lady of Saint-Germain-la-Rivière are therefore exceptional objects that could not be found in the immediate environment of the site. 'We believe that these were exotic objects that had come some distance', most certainly from much further south, or even beyond the Pyrenees, where forests still existed at that time and the climate was more temperate.

For Marian Vanhaeren, this provides an additional clue to the exceptional status of the deceased:

In traditional societies, exotic objects with standard-ized shapes always indicate prestige. The Lady of Saint-Germain-la-Rivière would therefore have had a special status, as indicated by her ornaments... These objects have been accumulated over time for her, to put them in her grave.

Professor Dani Nadel observed the same thing in the work-shops of the Ohalo site in Israel:

On the site we found hundreds of beads fashioned from two types of shell: one, called Dentalium, is a delicate shell that's as long as a matchstick. The craftsmen had cut it into strips. We also found pierced beads made from another type of shell called Columbella. These two spe-cies have never lived near Lake Tiberias, even during the last Ice Age. So we know that they were brought from the Mediterranean, and even from the Red Sea. This tells us that people, in this era, invested a lot of time and resources to make these beads from exotic raw materials. Maybe it's related to ornamentation... to women... But maybe it's not related to gender... Anyway, we found hundreds of them.

Were the women for whom the other members of the group had collected these jewels community leaders at that time? If so, could the Venus figurines be representations of these leaders? After all, history teaches us that powerful people like having their portraits made. Could this profusion of female art prove that some women occupied positions of leadership? Catherine Schwab wonders whether it is relevant to use artistic representations to assess the political importance of one particular gender within the group: 'Representations of women are much more numerous than representations of men. Extrapolating from that to imagine matriarchal societies with women leading the groups rather than men... this might be going a bit far.'

'The prime importance of female fertility for the survival of the group makes me think that humans created a matrilineal system,'* suggests Marylène Patou-Mathis, although she emphasizes the difficulty of the exercise because, she says, 'We have no evidence that allows us to talk about the widespread occurrence of matriarchy.'

Primitive matriarchy, a society in which women wield power, is a utopia that became associated with the image of prehistory in the 1970s, when feminist archaeologists became prominent in the discipline. For them, matriarchy was synonymous with a form of social organization that hardly ever engaged in conflict and was relatively egalitarian. Such a paradigm allowed these feminists to stand up to a system in which they felt bullied, and which they regarded as phallocratic and violent. In response, they were told that such matriarchal societies do not exist. The truth is more nuanced, since rare examples do exist, such as the Minangkabau people of Sumatra and the Yanzi in Zaire. Nevertheless, these matriarchal societies are very much in the minority among today's populations, both

---

* Unlike a patrilineal system, a social system is said to be matrilineal when maternal ancestry is predominant.

modern and traditional. But that does not prove that they could not have existed, or even have been dominant 30,000 or 15,000 years ago. Moreover, there is an interesting constant in African founding myths. Many of them say that in the earliest days of humanity, women had power over men. However, they were too curious, too strong or too warlike, and often made mistakes that made the gods distrust human beings. The situation therefore had to be reversed and women subjected to male authority so that order could be restored.

Whether the African elders are right or not, some argue that women had the opportunity of becoming powerful as the wife or daughter of the most influential man in the group. This is possible in some societies, but not in all, as Michèle Coquet explains: 'Among the Inuit, the leaders' women have a special status. But among hunter-gatherers, it is very rare for a marriage to be the driver of social recognition.'

Among hunter-gatherers, talent and expertise in a specific field seem to offer the main route to gaining higher status. And there is a field in which women were able to distinguish themselves very early on – early medical knowledge.

The Power of Healing

If women knew about the properties of plants, they may have been the founders of medicine.

Sophie A. de Beaune's comment highlights the fact that if we now have good reason to believe that women had particular expertise in selecting plants that could be used in food and for making everyday objects, we must also consider that they performed other, even more vital functions.

Indeed, plants form the basis of many treatments, from the first moisturisers to antiseptics essential for surviving infection. Dani Nadel found remains of non-food plants at the Ohalo site:

In addition to cereal seeds, we found seeds from medicinal plants at the site. So we've got food plants, edible fruits, species gathered for their therapeutic values, and perhaps even for their beauty.*

Using plants in this way 19,000 years ago does not surprise archaeologists, who have been able to show that Neanderthals were already using plant poultices to soothe toothache 49,000 years ago. In the El Sidrón Cave in Spain, an individual was treating an abscess on a tooth by chewing vegetable matter containing poplar buds, a rich source of salicylic acid – a natural form of aspirin. Scientists identified this cure by analysing the fossilized dental plaque of the 'patient' – a valuable source of information.

More recently, a whole medicine cabinet has been detected in the human coprolites found in the Pedra Furada rock shelter in Brazil. These fossilised faeces, around 8,000 years old, revealed that people were eating non-food plants probably ingested for pharmaceutical purposes. In the first-aid kit of Brazilian hunter-gatherers, there is something to cure all kinds of ailments. Bowel problems were treated by

---

* Tamarisk is very useful for treating wounds; thistle for soothing stomach aches; and sweet clover is known for its coagulating properties.

consuming anti-dysentery remedies extracted from trees such as *Caesalpinia* and *Terminalia*. The use of worming treatments derived from plants such as *Chenopodium* and *Bauhinia* has also been observed. And digestive problems could be relieved using an infusion of small plants with white flowers called *cabeça-de-velhô* ('old man's head'; *Borreria* spp.). Herbaceous plants of the Malvaceae family, the leaves of which may reduce infection in wounds, were also eaten, and leaves of the Embauba tree were used for pain relief. Lastly, respiratory tract problems were treated with *marmeleiro* or *velame* – the bark of the Anadenanthera tree (*angico* as it is called in Brazil), a powerful expectorant.

Closer to home, it is quite possible that the last Mesolithic hunter-gatherers in Scandinavia used betulin, which is found in birch tar, as a powerful antiseptic. This is what seems to have been revealed by the discovery made in December 2019 by scientists at the University of Copenhagen. In Denmark 5,700 years ago, a woman chewed a paste made from heated birch bark. Analysis of ancient DNA in her saliva revealed that she had infectious mononucleosis (glandular fever). It is possible that she also wanted to treat her various mouth problems, including herpes, again revealed by DNA markers. However, we should note that birch tar has been commonly used since the Middle Paleolithic as glue to attach flint shards to a handle or pole. This woman could therefore just as easily have been chewing this paste in order to soften it before applying it to a tool. This kind of chewing gum is not unique: another comparable discovery was made in Sweden in May 2019. At a Mesolithic site dating back more than 9,000 years and excavated in the late

1980s, Swedish archaeologists working in a pit discovered around a hundred of these dark-coloured pieces of chewing gum, the size of a thumb, covered in toothmarks. Chemical analysis of some of these pieces confirmed that they were indeed birch tar. Human DNA was identified in three of these samples, two female and one male. The size of the teeth, which could be estimated from the marks left on the gum, revealed that the 'chewers' were young and aged between five and eighteen.

In any case, it is very likely that prehistoric people were experts in using plants therapeutically, and it's possible that women, as guardians of the plant world, were humanity's first physicians.

Sometimes, there's a thin line between medicine and magic. Among many traditional populations, shamans and sorcerers are therapists first and foremost – and women are not excluded from these roles. In Central Asia, for example, women with a good knowledge of plants can become shamans when they are old. They use plants in healing, but also by applying magical objects and calling for the intervention of Muslim saints. This was the explanation given to ethnomusicologist Jean During by an eighty-year-old female shaman from southern Kazakhstan who took great pride in successfully using her knife on patients' wounds in order to relieve their pain.

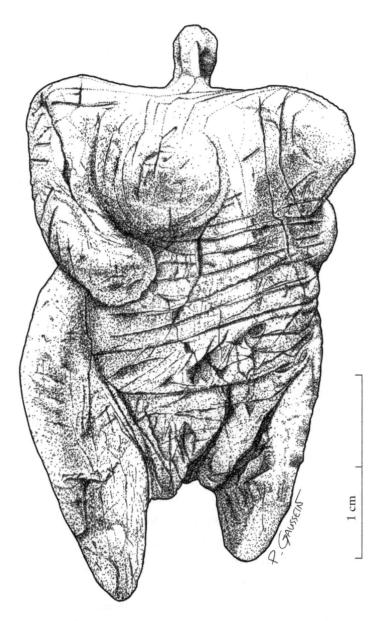

1 cm

The famous Venus of Hohle Fels (Germany), a small pendant
of a woman with a pronounced vulva and generous breasts.
Was she a prophylactic amulet?

Some archaeologists make the link between femininity and magic for medical use. Nicholas Conard likes to see the Venus figurine pendant found in Hohle Fels, Germany as having functions related to magic and obstetrics:

> *I imagine that carrying this item of jewellery on one's person might make women feel more confident when dealing with pregnancy, which involves a radical change in the body, and also with childbirth, which is a major event for the group.*

It's hard to imagine that a source of magical power applied to the female world and childbirth did not belong to women with empirical knowledge of parturition. Nevertheless Nicolas Conard remains cautious:

> *I'm speculating, of course, but I'm inclined to believe that this figurine was made by a woman, worn by a woman and handed down from generation to generation. Knowledge associated with human reproduction and childbirth, as well as other aspects of fertility in the broadest sense, could have been handed down with this object.*

From this perspective, what about the evidence found in prehistoric excrement of traces of the tropical 'pau ferro' tree [*Libidibia ferrea*] whose fruits, taken as an infusion, can induce abortion? Brazilian women in the 8th millennium BCE may have whispered this secret to each other down the generations as a way of regulating the birth rate.

For prehistorians, it seems very natural to imagine women doctors, and the same ought to be the case for magical and religious functions, since the latter often go hand in hand with knowledge of apothecary remedies. However, prehistoric shamanism has always been associated with men – the fault, perhaps, of some very rare representations of male figures (there are less than ten of them) whose bulging eyes seem to gaze towards an invisible world. We can see this, for example, in the half-man, half-animal creature traditionally called the Sorcerer who was found in the Cave of the Trois-Frères in the Ariège département, and has been dated to the Magdalenian era between 17,000 and 10,000 BCE.

The Sorceror cave painting in the Cave of the Trois- Frères, Ariège, stares at us with bulging eyes.

This anthropomorphic figure with the ears and antlers of a deer stands upright in a theatrical pose. Bearded, he sports a ponytail and oddly positioned male genitalia. It is possible that these attributes are artificial, just like the antler headdress. So why should we not imagine a young woman who is an expert in the plant world wearing this ritualistic costume? Francesco d'Errico does not rule out the possibility that women may have been in contact with invisible powers:

In some Siberian populations, women were shamans: they could communicate with the dead and cure illnesses. Data such as those found in the tomb at Saint-Germain-la-Rivière seem to point in this direction... Nothing precludes us from thinking that the women of the Upper Paleolithic could have occupied social roles equivalent to those of men in the realm of rituals, as in all other areas of social life.

Indeed, the connection between women and shamanism is well-known in social anthropology and can be seen particularly among the Nenets people of Russia and the Buryats of Mongolia. In these communities, women play the drums and make offerings of yak milk to make contact with gods, ghosts and ancestors.

So prehistoric women were able to intercede between humans and the gods – a magical power, which, for some, suggests that the first forms of spirituality may have emerged in the darkness of the subterranean world. For others, cave art is linked to a mythology concerning the animal world. But this is all very speculative: the journey of the male – or female – shaman is essentially a journey of the spirit and does not leave fossil traces.

What then of the hundreds of Venus figurines carved from ivory, bone or clay? Could these be the first gods worshipped by our ancestors?

What if God Was a Woman?

Admittedly, very little is known about the spiritual life of our Paleolithic ancestors. Passed down from generation to generation through oral traditions, their beliefs have been lost in the mists of time. While artists may have represented their pantheon on the walls of caves and rock shelters using engraving and painting, the keys to understanding these works remain a mystery.

Are these powerful animals, these hybrid, half-human, half-animal figures and these pneumatic women who float across the walls depictions of the beings who, for our ancestors, ruled the world? Are they totems, shamanic visions, the representation of ancestors or nature spirits? The symbolic power of these prehistoric works of art still remains beyond our comprehension.

When trying to identify a deity, you need to know its attributes. Indeed, the gods bear symbols that enable the faithful to recognize them, and female figures are often associated with certain representational invariants. We recall the extent to which sexual characteristics and motherhood are highlighted in the Paleolithic Venus figurines: the rounded belly, the linea nigra typical of pregnant women, and breasts that are sometimes swollen to signify ongoing breastfeeding, sometimes sagging to indicate breastfeeding in the past. Were these women fertility figures? Could the famous 'mother goddess', which some archaeologists believe they have identified in the Neolithic female figures, have its roots in the Paleolithic era?

The engraved frescoes at Roc-aux-Sorciers might suggest that woman was a symbolic figure linked to managing fertility in human groups, maybe to the extent of being a goddess of love and reproduction – both Venus and Gaia. Catherine Schwab has carried out a detailed study of these Venus figurines with their rounded bellies:

> *There are figurines of women who are about to give birth, for example those found at Balzi Rossi near Grimaldi. These are images of pregnant women, representations of this episode in the lives of women... Focusing on this must mean something.*

However, interpreting prehistoric Venus figurines as the 'mother goddess' is not very popular among young archaeologists. The thesis put forward for decades by the American prehistorian Marija Gimbutas is now widely disputed. Professor Randall White explains how our interpretations are influenced by our own era:

> *These objects speak to us, but in a language that we find it difficult to interpret. The kinds of questions we ask them are imbued with concerns that mirror our time. In France, after the First World War, we suddenly began to see these representations of women as symbols of fertility.*

We have to relocate this interpretation in its temporal context: at that time, the government was launching a major programme to boost the birth rate. So many men had been killed during the war that the role of women became explicitly one of reproduction. It is probably no coincidence that the mother goddess was very popular during this time.

These efforts to contextualize research historically are necessary to assess the influence of the mentalities of one's own era and the effects of fashion on prehistory. It is likely that the current rejection of the prehistoric mother goddess theory is also representative of our time, perhaps because after hundreds of years of having been seen as a womb, women today have grown tired of being identified with childbirth. However, representing woman as mother does not mean underestimating her role in society. On the contrary, 'parturition is not a handicap or a curse', as Oscar Fuentes stresses forcefully. 'This is a moment of female power since the other half of humanity is not able to bear life.'

In the Museum of Prehistory at Blaubeuren in Germany, which is home to some of the oldest everyday objects belonging to Upper Paleolithic hunter-gatherers and some of humankind's earliest artistic treasures, scientist Nicholas Conard focuses in particular on the Venus of Hohle Fels. For him, she is symbolic of the divine power of women:

We are in the most important exhibition room in the museum, the one where the female figurine of Hohle Fels is on show. It was found in summer 2008 at an archaeo-logical site just a few kilometres from here. It's the ideal place to consider questions of art, female identity and the role of women in the history of humankind.

When he describes the Venus of Hohle Fels, Conard admits that he has to contain his enthusiasm, so that he doesn't spend a full half-hour detailing the morphology of the greatest treasure he has excavated: 'She was carved from mammoth ivory. The characteristics leave no room for doubt: the breasts, the vulva. We are indeed looking at a woman.'

In the case of this Venus, the head is missing, and this is not the only part of the body that has been overlooked: 'The legs are practically non-existent.' For Nicholas Conard, these characteristics clearly demonstrate the artist's desire to represent much more than just one person: 'When you depict an individual, their face matters. In this case, it's not about an individual or about movement: everything evokes reproduction, the very essence of woman.'

Nicholas Conard emphasizes that this is 'certainly not a realistic portrayal' because prehistoric women were not that plump – at least not the majority of them. However, the standards of beauty that value large women vary greatly from society to society: such images are often a sign of a certain degree of prosperity, while the current appeal of waif-like figures in women is very recent. This is indeed what Catherine Schwab points out:

In many earlier civilizations, a very plump woman showed that she had enough to eat. It signified a certain degree of affluence. We can imagine finding this type of criteria in Paleolithic populations. Motherhood also had to be taken into account. By showcasing these women whose bodies bear the signs of multiple pregnancies, the artists may have wanted to represent a symbol of the group's continuity and the continuity of humanity more generally… why not!

Nicholas Conard believes that these muses were even able to symbolize fertility in the broadest sense, that is in the animal and plant world: 'Of course, human reproduction is essential for the group's survival, but it's essential especially throughout nature – in plants and animals. Everything around us is about life and reproduction and it's essential for survival during the Ice Age.'

Despite the powerful sexual attributes of the Venus of Hohle Fels, Nicholas Conard absolutely does not accept that this can be interpreted as an erotic figure. For him, the prehistoric woman with her generous curves 'is an analogy of the world our ancestors lived in. She carries within her the animal and plant kingdom, the cycle of the seasons.' In short, she symbolizes the universe.

For our female ancestors, this hypothesis is particularly attractive and empowering. However, Emeritus Professor Denis Vialou warns us against the temptation to generalize:

We must not interpret these prehistoric Venus figurines within an absolutist framework […]. The concept of 'mother goddess' that has been attributed to them is essentially linked to the history of these finds. The uniformity of these figurines is our own invention.

For Vialou, it seems dangerous to imagine that a divine figure could persist over several millennia without these ideas being handed down through writing.

Other experts don't share this opinion. For them, it is quite possible that these statuettes are representations of goddesses, and that the same discourse circulated across large geographical areas. Some even imagine that the Venus figurines were at the heart of very special religious rituals. In Nicholas Conard's opinion, this might have been the case with the Venus of Hohle Fels, as it was found lying below the oldest level of the first human occupation of the cave.

Maybe this group dug a hole for the Venus. When we found it, the female figurine of Hohle Fels was at the bottom of the Aurignacian archaeological level (38,000 years ago). This period coincides with the arrival of modern humans in Europe. We found the figurine by digging below this Aurignacian stratigraphic layer.

Similar figurines found in pits dug inside the living area have also been unearthed at two Russian sites, Avdeevo and Kostenki I. Could this act of burial be the oldest evidence of rituals practised in accordance with ancestral beliefs? It is interesting to note that some artists intentionally produced fragments of female bodies. But why would they represent parts of a body?

Some scientists believe that this is the representation of a myth: the myth of a fragmented goddess whose epic tale is re-enacted in the semi-darkness of cave sanctuaries. The historian and philosopher Michel Serres pointed out that many mythological stories feature gods that have been dismembered. From the cosmogony of the Dogon people to the mythology of the Marind-Anim of New Guinea and the Egypt of the pharaohs, mythical scenes in which bodies are cut up, buried in separate places or scattered around the world are almost a religious invariant. Are we then looking at proof of the existence of a very ancient mythical figure?

The simplest and most probable hypothesis is that artists very often chose to use the part to represent the whole, that is to say they used metonyms* to represent men, women and animals. Thus ibex horns stand for the animal itself, a mane for the horse, broad palmated antlers for the megaloceros [an extinct genus of giant deer], the dorsal line with its characteristic hump for the mammoth, the erect phallus for man, and finally the vulva and breasts for woman.

The Origin of the World

Other prehistoric representations of women seem to have a mythological aspect. This is what Boris Valentin, Professor at the Panthéon-Sorbonne University in Paris, maintains, since he and his team carried out a study of an engraving of a female form found in the middle of the Forest of Fontainebleau.

Three slits were carved by human hand, emphasizing

---

* Metonym is a figure of speech in which a concept is referred to using a term designating a second concept that is closely related to the former.

the naturally suggestive triangular shape of the rock. The rounded ceiling of this cavity suggests a plump belly, and on each side of the pubis two raised blocks evoke thighs upon which two galloping horses are depicted. The style of the depiction of these horses enables us to date the creation of this engraving to some 20,000 years ago.

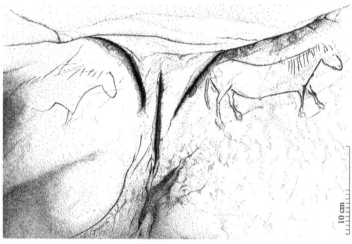

The Origin of the World – *Paleolithic style – in the Forest of Fontainebleau, Seine-et- Marne.*

This artwork was created at the end of a narrow passageway that suggests the journey of a baby being born. The archaeological team's latest observations show that, during heavy rain, water flows naturally along the central slit, perhaps suggesting waters breaking just before birth.

For Professor Valentin, this is a Paleolithic version of Gustave Courbet's famous painting *The Origin of the World*. Like a founding myth, prehistoric woman would be seen as the original matrix through which the world would have been born – a kind of Stone Age cosmogony.

Afterword

LADY SAPIENS – OUR CLOSE RELATIVE

It is often at the end of a lengthy project that we begin to think again about the beginning. In spring 2018, when we had just completed our first scientific investigation into the disappearance of the Neanderthals, the archaeological world began announcing a stream of new discoveries about the origins of *Homo sapiens*. In light of this news, we naturally thought, together with Jacques Malaterre, of working on a new history of mankind. And it was then that inspiration struck. Wasn't it time to take a different route? What if, beyond the remarkable summary work written on the subject, we were to attempt the very first field study to breathe new life not into early man but into Ice Age woman? We were determined to explore this new history of man, but this time revealing the hidden life of his inseparable other half.

Our meeting with prehistorian Sophie A. de Beaune was crucial. She agreed to be our scientific advisor, both on the film *Lady Sapiens*, which our producer Sophie Parrault (of documentary film company Little Big Story) very quickly supported, and on the book you are about to finish reading. She placed her trust in us by sharing with us her groundbreaking work, then being published by Oxford University Press. It's a fascinating study focusing in particular on the distribution of tasks between men and women in the Upper Paleolithic. We were then able to assess the enormous potential of the subject that lay before us, and we decided to go even further by interviewing contemporary scientists in order to bring Lady Sapiens back to life.

We are now able to offer a recreation of Lady Sapiens's daily life as you have just discovered, and can state, beyond our own personal conviction, that our prehistoric female ancestors were essential to their clan's survival. This has come as a result of our investigations in the laboratories of paleogeneticists, prehistorians and paleoanthropologists; after dangerous explorations of obscure passageways in decorated caves where we examined the walls and the ancient soil in search of the slightest clue; after meeting with the scientists who deciphered in detail the female figurines known as 'Venus' and looked under the microscope at archaeological remains made of perishable material that until now had been invisible; and after many discussions with ethnologists specializing in the last hunter-gatherer peoples and their environment.

This factual investigation into the day-to-day activities of female *sapiens* in the Upper Paleolithic will, hopefully, put an end to a number of recurring clichés. The objects unearthed by archaeologists speak to us and ultimately reveal a Lady Sapiens who occupies more than the single role of nurturer, a sensitive woman who is concerned about her appearance, a talented craftswoman, who is independent and autonomous in the production of her daily tools, and a provider of food essential to the survival of her group. As for her participation in hunting, an activity less essential than the predominant approach has led us to believe, there is no longer any doubt:

some women in the Upper Paleolithic, like men, threw spears to kill big game, and most likely took part in less dangerous hunting strategies. Above all, we know that Lady Sapiens knew how to process meat products.

The scientists we met around the world, in Europe, the Middle East and the United States, agree on the fundamental place of women within the group. A complementary combination of disciplines – sometimes completely unexpected, such as the meeting of archeologists and Namibian trackers who were seeking the source of the thousand-year-old footprints in the clay soil of the excavated world – now enables us to refine our understanding of the different roles women occupied in ancient times: artists, medical pioneers who understood the plant world, respected and even celebrated figures. We can echo the comment by Henry de Lumley: 'The Lady of Cavillon must have had a special status, since she was given an exceptional burial… The crucial question is, what was it?'

We may never know if the women buried in such privileged ways were shamans, leaders or leaders' wives. But it is highly likely that, in the decades to come, science will eventually lift the veil on questions that remain unanswered at the present time, especially as the tools available to scientists are constantly improving.

Research Perspectives

Improvements in physico-chemical analyses will enable us to delve deeper and deeper into the personal lives of our ancestors and unravel their secrets. Like the bond between mother and baby, who would have imagined a few years ago that it would be possible to identify the weaning age of *Homo erectus* babies and their successors by studying, as Vincent Balter did in his Lyon laboratory, the isotopic signatures of dental enamel?

Thanks to paleogenetics, ancient DNA will soon have even more to tell us about our parentage, our ways of meeting, our interbreeding. We can now learn about the family ties of the individuals who were buried together, as well as the evolution of their physical appearance. We can hope to detect with more certainty how tasks were shared between men and women by carrying out more and more analyses of human remains. Although in the past the contamination of samples with modern DNA has deprived us of a lot of data, this is now a much rarer occurrence, since for at least a decade paleo-geneticists have been operating on site and taking samples under optimal conditions, thus preventing any contamination. Increasingly, all these advances are allowing us to answer questions that are currently unresolved and will continue to do so.

Advances in the precision of dating methods will allow scientists to establish an ever more sophisticated chronology of human developments in art and technology.

New archaeological discoveries are awaiting us on sites that have remained unexplored or are still unknown.

Another avenue seems promising for understanding what made us human beings. Research into the origin of our social behaviours shows that our evolution owes more to our life choices within a community than to technical innovations, as Jean-Jacques Hublin emphasizes:

The work of Sarah Hrdy and other anthropologists is very important, because it has shifted the spotlight away from technical progress and towards the type of progress that is not only social but above all behavioural.

Thus, an apparently innocuous phenomenon can reveal mechanisms linked to the evolution of our way of life within a community.

There is an evolutionary pressure that fosters altruism and empathy, because, in fact, these ancestral groups must not have been the site of very many conflicts. The most violent individuals, those who killed others, captured their wives – I'm talking about the males obviously – well, they were forced out, even eliminated. This generated changes, not only in behaviour, but also in morphology: over the course of recent evolution, our physical features have become more and more friendly. Characteristics such as the supra-orbital ridge – very pronounced eyebrow arches, a powerful trait observed in ancient hominins – have disappeared to be replaced by very mobile eyebrows which enable a whole range of expressions and emotions. All of this works towards an improved ability to read the minds of others, communicate with them and develop empathy.

This evolution in community life necessarily had repercussions on relationships between men and women, and created a new social model that Sarah Hrdy and Jean-Jacques Hublin describe as 'cooperative'. Consequently, young children no longer belong to one single woman, since now the whole group devotes attention to them and cares for them, which will increase their chances of survival.

Today, these new focuses are shifting the centre of gravity in research. Hunting or technological innovations are no longer the only fields of investigation, and the role of ancestral women occupies an essential and fundamental place in these studies.

New developments are therefore to be expected. The scientists of today and tomorrow will pave the way for an ever deeper understanding of the origin of our shared humanity. Lady Sapiens' adventures are beginning to emerge before our very eyes.

Cultural Variations

During this investigation, many scientists emphasized the fact that each population living in Europe during the Upper Paleolithic was unique. While it is possible that symbols and images circulated among the different groups, it is unlikely that these groups shared the same social organization. Therefore we cannot make generalizations about women's roles from the study of a single archaeological site. Marian Vanhaeren urges us to keep our speculation open to notions of diversity:

Different types of organization have necessarily existed, depending on the place and the era. Role reversals could certainly have occurred at certain times for a variety of reasons. Our view of prehistory should be extremely varied.

'Even today, in different regions of the world, the status of women is not at all the same everywhere. And it must have been like this in the past.' The common sense expressed in this comment by José Braga should guide our approach to the question.

Making Progress Together while Respecting Individuality

During the Upper Paleolithic, individualism could only have meant danger. In these groups comprising between some twenty to a hundred people, each member had to participate in the life of the community. Everyone was responsible for the group's progress and undertakings. The first representatives of humanity worked together to create diverse and subtle cultures. As Dani Nadel argues, 'our ancestors lived together. Every idea, every success, every failure and every invention was the product of the group.'

Nadel does not imagine that these human groups with limited demographics could have thought any differently.

His colleagues argue that individual talent and individual tastes had to be taken into account when assigning different tasks. Human groups were governed by more or less strict rules of conduct, but it is probable that the most challenging tasks requiring a particular skill, such as stone-working or decorating the walls of caves, were entrusted to the most talented individuals, regardless of gender.

Yesterday's Woman – Today's Woman

As Évelyne Heyer emphasizes, studying prehistoric societies and today's hunter-gatherer populations shows us that there is no predetermined destiny and that the range of possibilities is surely wider than we imagine. Evolution does not follow a singular path.

Studying the past and present teaches us that there is not just one path taken by human societies. The latter can follow divergent routes [...]. Ultimately, we cannot envision a single route that all the societies of the past would have followed, in which they would transition, step by step, from one kind of social organization to another, as people believed in the early twentieth century.

It is likely that the women of the Upper Paleolithic were not much different from women today. Generous, skilful, daring and determined: the qualities embodied by our grandmothers, mothers and sisters were already embedded in Lady Sapiens's DNA.

Michèle Coquet suggests we take an idealized look at this community of women, all united around the same aspiration, namely to find happiness for themselves, but also to help create the happiness of others.

I would think that what I observed in anthropological studies already worked for prehistory: in particular I saw a high degree of solidarity between women. From little girls to grandmothers, they are united by the necessary bonds of mutual aid... and in an intimate way.

This kind of female solidarity should not make us forget that together men and women were involved in a human adventure that required the effort of everyone. The scientists we interviewed during this project such as Claudine Karlin regularly emphasized this collective aspect:

We need this complementary relationship between men and women in order to survive, and I think that for pre-historic people it was the same: men and women need one another.

It is not for science to decide if women are the future of men, but it is clear that women have created their past to a considerable extent. From now on, it is up to each of us, both women and men as individuals, to decide which role we wish to play in shaping the world of tomorrow.

Thanks to the tenacious work of archaeologists and the multitude of clues they have amassed, Lady Sapiens can finally emerge from the shadows, freed from the burden of prejudice. Rediscovering her voice, her footsteps and her gestures allows us to rediscover the history of our origins – a sensitive and fairer history of women and men, united in a common destiny of which we are the heirs.

Thomas Cirotteau and Éric Pincas

Select Bibliography

Women in prehistory: general works

Beaune, Sophie A. de and Antoine Balzeau. *Notre préhistoire. La grande aventure de la famille humaine*, Belin, 2016. Berrouet, Florian and Alexandre Hurel. *Femmes: naissance de l'homme. Icônes de la Préhistoire*, Quai des Brunes, 'Le Temps des femmes', 2018.

Hrdy, Sarah Blaffer. *La femme qui n'évoluait jamais*, Payot, 'Petite Bibliothèque Payot', 2002.

Comment nous sommes devenus humains. Les origines de l'empathie, L'Instant présent, 2016.

Cohen, Claudine. *Femmes de la Préhistoire*, Belin, 2016; Tallandier, 'Texto', 2021.

La Femme des origines. Images de la femme dans la Préhistoire occidentale, Belin-Herscher, 2003.

Patou-Mathis, Marylène. *L'homme préhistorique est aussi une femme. Une histoire de l'invibilité des femmes*, Allary, 2020.

Homo sapiens and their ancestors: a biological approach

Collective. *Vénus et Caïn. Figures de la Préhistoire, 1830–1930*. RMN, 2003.

Heyer, Évelyne. *L'Odyssée des gènes*, Flammarion, 2020.

(ed.). *Une belle histoire de l'homme*, Éditions du musée de l'Homme/Flammarion, 2015.

Hublin, Jean-Jacques and Bernard Seytre. *Quand d'autres hommes peuplaient la Terre. Nouveaux regards sur nos origines*, Flammarion, 'Champs Sciences', 2011.

Hunter-gatherers

Bahuchet, Serge. *Les Pygmées Aka et la forêt centrafricaine*, SELAF-CNRS, 1985.

Clastres, Pierre. *Chroniques des Indiens Guayaki*, Plon, 'Terre Humaine', 1972.

Gessain, Robert. *Ammassalik ou la civilisation obligatoire*, Flammarion, 1969.

Sahlins, Marshall. *Stone Age Economics*, Routledge, 2017.

Thomas, Elizabeth Marshall. *The Harmless People*, Random House, 1959.

Testart, Alain. *Essai sur les fondements de la division sexuelle du travail chez les chasseurs-cueilleurs*, EHESS, 1986.

Sex and osteology

Braga, José et al. 'Cochlear Shape Reveals that the Human Organ of Hearing Is Sex-Typed from Birth', *Scientific Reports*, (2019), vol. 9, no 1.

Murail, Pascal et al. 'DSP: A Tool for Probabilistic Sex Diagnosis Using Worldwide Variability in Hip-Bone Measurements', *Bulletins et mémoires de la Société d'anthropologie de Paris*, (2005), vol. 17, nos. 3–4, pp. 167–76.

Nomadism, food, physical activities: prehistoric ways of life

Beaune, Sophie A. de *Chasseurs-cueilleurs. Comment vivaient nos ancêtres du Paléolithique supérieur*, CNRS Éditions, 'Biblis', 2013.

Beaune, Sophie A. de. 'A Critical Analysis of the Evidence for Sexual Division of Tasks in the European Upper Paleolithic' in K.A. Overmann and F.L. Coolidge (eds.), *Squeezing Minds from Stones: Cognitive Archeology and the Evolution of the Human Mind*, Oxford University Press, 2019, pp. 376–405.

Julien, Michèle and Claudine Karlin (eds.). *Un automne à Pincevent. Le campement magdalénien du niveau IV20*, Société préhistorique française, 2014.

Molleson, Theya Ivitsky. 'The Eloquent Bones of Abu Hureyra', *Scientific American*, (1994), vol. 271, no. 2, pp. 70–75.

Meehan, Courtney L. and Alyssa N. Crittenden (eds.). *Childhood: Origins, Evolution, and Implications*, University of New Mexico Press, 2016.

Owen, Linda R. *Distorting the Past: Gender and the Division of Labor in the European Upper Paleolithic*, Kerns Verlag, 2005.

Tacail, Théo et al. 'Assessing Human Weaning Practices with Calcium Isotopes in Tooth Enamel', *PNAS* (2017), vol. 114, no. 24, pp. 6268–6273.

Valentin, Boris. *Le Paléolithique*, PUF, 'Que sais-je ?', 2019.

Villotte, Sébastien. 'Enthésopathies et activités des hommes préhistoriques. Recherche méthodologique et application aux fossiles européens du Paléolithique supérieur et du Mésolithique' (Ph.D. thesis, Biological Anthropology, University of Bordeaux I, 2008); published by British Archaeological Reports, Archaeopress, 2009.

Villotte, Sébastien et al. 'The Paleobiology of Two Adult Skeletons from Baousso da Torre (Bausu da Ture) (Liguria,

Italy): Implications for Gravettian Lifestyle', *Comptes rendus Palevol*, (2017), vol. 16, no. 4, pp. 462–473.

Art and craft

Adovasio, James M., Olga Soffer and Jake Page. *The Invisible Sex: Uncovering the True Roles of Women in Prehistory*, Routledge, 2009.

Adovasio, James M. 'The Appearance of Plant Fiber Artifacts: An Upper Paleolithic Event Horizon', paper presented to the symposium 'Going Beyond Stone Tools: The Other Signs of Paleolithic Transitions', 17th international conference of the International Union of Prehistoric and Protohistoric Sciences, Florianopolis, Brazil, 2011.

Dupuy, Delphine. 'Fragments d'images, images de fragments. La statuaire gravettienne, du geste au symbole' (Ph.D. thesis, Archaeology and Prehistory, University of Provence – Aix-Marseille I, 2007).

Paris, Clément et al. 'Premières observations sur le gisement gravettien à statuettes féminines d'Amiens-Renancourt 1 (Somme)', *Bulletin de la Société préhistorique française*, (2017), vol. 114, no. 3, pp. 423–444.

Vanhaeren, Marian and Francesco d'Errico. 'Aurignacian Ethno-Linguistic Geography of Europe Revealed by Personal Ornaments', *Journal of Archaeological Science*, (2006), vol. 33, no. 8, pp. 1105–1128.

Relationships and sexuality

Alvarez, Helen Perich. 'Grandmother Hypothesis and Primate Life Histories', *Physical Anthropology*, (2000), vol. 113, no. 3, pp. 435–450.

Bozinski, Gerhard. *Femmes sans tête. Une icône culturelle dans l'Europe de la fin de l'ère glaciaire*, Errance, 2011.

Brody, Benjamin. 'The Sexual Significance of the Axillae', *Psychiatry*, (1975), vol. 38, no. 3, pp. 278–289.

Buisson-Catil, Jacques and Jérôme Primault. *Le Roc-aux-Sorciers. Rencontre avec le peuple magdalénien*, Association des publications chauvinoises, 2012.

Delluc, Brigitte, Gilles Delluc and Jean-Pierre Duhard (eds.). *Représentation de l'intimité féminine dans l'art paléolithique en France*, Presses universitaires de Liège, 2017.

Delluc, Gilles. *Le Sexe au temps des Cro-Magnons*, Pilote, 2006.

Hayden, Brian. *L'Homme et l'Inégalité. L'invention de la hiérarchie durant la Préhistoire*, CNRS Éditions, 'Le passé recomposé', 2008.

Hublin, Jean-Jacques. *Biologie de la culture. Paléoanthropologie du genre Homo*, Collège de France/Fayard, 2017.

Iakovleva, Ludmila and Geneviève Pinçon. 'La frise sculptée du Roc-aux-Sorciers', *Bulletin de la Société préhistorique française*, (1998), vol. 95, no. 1, pp. 110–111.

Kim, Peter S., James E. Coxworth and Kristen Hawkes. 'Increased Longevity Evolves from Grandmothering', *Proceedings of the Royal Society B: Biological Sciences*, (2012), vol. 279, no. 1749, pp. 4880–4884.

Kirshenbaum, Sheril. *The Science of Kissing: What Our Lips Are Telling Us*, Grand Central Publishing, 2011.

Lahdenperä, M., V. Lummaa and A. F. Russell. 'Menopause: Why Does Fertility End Before Life?', *Climacteric*, (2004), vol. 7, no. 4, pp. 327–331.

Lumley, Henry de. *La Grotte du Cavillon sous la falaise Baousse Rousse Grimaldi, Vintimille, Italie*, CNRS Éditions, 2016.

Picq, Pascal. *Et l'évolution créa la femme*, Odile Jacob, 2020.

Picq, Pascal and Philippe Brenot. *Le Sexe, l'Homme et l'Évolution*, Odile Jacob, 2009.

Svoboda, Jiří A. and Dolní Věstonice-Pavlov. *Explaining Paleolithic Settlements in Central Europe*, Texas A&M University Press, 2020.

Taylor, Timothy. *The Prehistory of Sex: Four Million Years of Human Sexual Culture*, Bantam, 1997.

Trinkaus, Erik. 'The Adiposity Paradox in the Middle Danubian Gravettian', *Anthropologie*, (2005), vol. 43, nos. 2–3, pp. 263–271.

About the Authors

Dr Jennifer Kerner teaches Prehistory in the anthropology department at Paris-Nanterre University, is responsible for multimedia communications at CNRS (National Centre for Scientific Research) and is an associate researcher at the National Museum of Natural History (Paris) and the Museum of Humankind (Paris).

Thomas Cirotteau is an author and director. He created and co-wrote the documentary *Lady Sapiens*. He also directed the documentary *Who Killed the Neanderthal?*, which he co-wrote with Eric Pincas and Jacques Malaterre. This film received a number of prizes in France and abroad.

Eric Pincas is a historian and journalist. He co-wrote the documentary *Lady Sapiens*, is editor-in-chief at *Historia* magazine since 2014, and has authored *Who Killed the Neanderthal?* (Michalon, 2014) and *Prehistory* (Perrin, 2020). He also co-wrote the documentary *Who Killed the Neanderthal?*.